birds

An **EXPLORE
YOUR WORLD**™
Handbook

DISCOVERY COMMUNICATIONS
Founder, Chairman, and Chief Executive Officer:
John S. Hendricks
President and Chief Operating Officer:
Judith A. McHale
President, Discovery Enterprises Worldwide:
Michela English

DISCOVERY PUBLISHING
Vice President, Publishing: Ann-Marie McGowan
Publishing Director: Natalie Chapman
Editorial Director: Rita Thievon Mullin
Senior Editor: Mary Kalamaras

DISCOVERY CHANNEL RETAIL
Product Development: Tracy Fortini
Naturalist: Steve Manning

DISCOVERY COMMUNICATIONS, INC., produces high-quality television programming, interactive media, books, films, and consumer products.
DISCOVERY NETWORKS, a division of Discovery Communications, Inc., operates and manages Discovery Channel, TLC, Animal Planet, and Travel Channel.

Birds, An Explore Your World ™ Handbook, was created and produced for DISCOVERY PUBLISHING by ST. REMY MEDIA INC.

Library of Congress Cataloging-in-Publication Data
Birds: an explore your world handbook.
    p.   cm.
    Includes bibliographical references (p.   ).
    ISBN 1-56331-800-8 (pbk.)
    1. Birds. 2. Bird watching. I. Discovery Channel (Firm)   II. Title: Birds.
    QL676.D57   1999
    598--dc21   99-24585
                                                          CPI

Random House website address:
http://www.atrandom.com
Discovery Channel Online website address:
http://www.discovery.com
Printed in the United States of America on acid-free paper
First Edition   10 9 8 7 6 5 4 3 2 1

CONSULTANTS

David M. Bird is a professor of wildlife biology and Director of the Avian Science and Conservation Centre of McGill University in Montreal. During his career, Dr. Bird has produced more than one hundred scientific papers on birds of prey. He has also edited or written several books on birds and is a regular columnist for *The Montreal Gazette* and *Bird Watcher's Digest.*

Jim Berry has been a professional interpretive naturalist for twenty-six years, working at the local, state, and national levels. Currently he is the president of the Roger Tory Peterson Institute of Natural History in Jamestown, New York.

Steve Kress is a research biologist for the National Audubon Society and Manager of the Society's Maine Coast Seabird Sanctuaries. He is also a Research Fellow at Cornell University, an Associate of the Cornell Laboratory of Ornithology, and an adjunct faculty member of the Wildlife Department at the University of Maine, Orono. Dr. Kress is the author of *Bird Garden* and the Golden Guide *Birdlife.*

Bill Thompson, III is the editor of *Bird Watcher's Digest* and the author of *Bird Watching for Dummies.* He has been an avid birdwatcher for more than twenty-five years.

NATURALIST PAINTER

Ghislain Caron is a Montreal-born naturalist painter whose original works have appeared in magazines, books, and galleries since he was a teenager. He was the exclusive illustrator of *Guide des Oiseaux du Québec et des Maritimes*, an artistic undertaking in the tradition of Roger Tory Peterson to which he devoted two years.

birds

An EXPLORE
YOUR WORLD™
Handbook

DISCOVERY BOOKS
NEW YORK

CONTENTS

DISCOVERING BIRDS

UNDER THE FEATHERS

Feathers may be their defining feature, but birds wouldn't be birds without a myriad of anatomical adaptations that enable them to flourish in their particular world. From the structure of birds' beaks to the design of their feet, there is a lot going on under the feathers.

A hawk wheels overhead, riding a thermal ever higher into the sky; a tiny hummingbird hovers next to a flower, its wings a blur—bird flight comes in an array of awe-inspiring guises. But the true miracle of flight lies in how it is even possible in the first place.

The story begins out of view, under the feathers. Birds are vertebrates like humans. Their skeletons contain all the basic parts found in human anatomy: a bony framework featuring a spinal column, rib cage, skull, and limbs. The bird's skeleton performs many of the same functions as the human frame, protecting vital organs, aiding locomotion, and manufacturing blood cells. But the similarities end there. In every detail, the bird skeleton has evolved in response to the challenge of flight.

The Dinosaur Connection

In 1861 a Bavarian farmer unearthed *Archaeopteryx*, a 150-million-year-old dinosaur fossil with feathered airfoil wings. Since then, debate over the origins of birds has raged.

The discovery of other fossils indicates that the ancestry of birds—and flight—involved more than feathers. Body structure, metabolism, social structure, and lifestyle all changed as animals took to the air. Recently, spectacular finds in China have strengthened the dinosaur-bird link by documenting the emergence of flight-related physical features. *Velociraptor* was a successful ground-dwelling predator with uniquely flexible wrist bones similar to the wing bones of later flying birds. *Caudipteryx* was a ground-dwelling runner that possessed a lightly toothed beak and tail feathers. A third discovery—a 120-million-year-old *Protoarchaeopteryx*—had the earliest known feathers for gliding.

Today more than a hundred shared features link birds and dinosaurs. Paleontologists are still far from developing a detailed avian family tree, but they have established that the ancestry of birds reaches back to small, dynamic carnivores who lived on the ground and slowly evolved the skills—and the bodies—to fill new niches in the trees and, ultimately, in the vast expanse of the skies.

To live on land and in the air, birds have developed a light-weight, strong, and compact bone struc-ture. Many bones, such as the heavy jaws, have been eliminated outright. Others, the tiny bones of the hand, for example, have been simplified or fused with others to create greater rigidity where it is needed. In most birds, virtually all bones are hol-low—a tremendous saving in weight that helps make flight possible. The skeleton of a frigatebird, a seabird that sports a seven-foot wingspan, actually weighs less than its feathers. However ingenious, this system is of no use to diving birds, such as the loon, that prize ballast over buoyancy. The bones of divers are mostly solid, which makes them heavy and less efficient for flying, but better suited for use underwater.

"It's not only fine feathers that make fine birds."

— *Aesop*

Bird bones are not only light, they are also unusually strong. Though hollow, they feature mazes of interior trusses, minute triangular struts, that keep them from snapping under the stress of wing beats. But strong bones are only the beginning. To enable flight, they have to be arranged in the right way. The enlarged breast provides several effective solutions. It achieves great rigidity through fused ribs and a latticework of tiny slatlike bones that reinforce the rib cage   front and back—at acute angles. These tiny bones not only

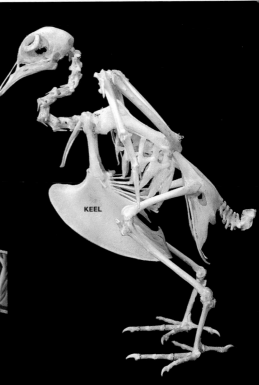

Right: *A substantial protruding keel dominates the skeleton of a pigeon. The keel provides birds with a large area for attachment of the well-developed wing muscles that make flight possible.*

KEEL

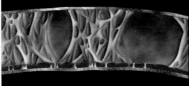

Above: *Most bird bones are hollow, a weight-saving compromise that assists flight. This hollow bone from an eagle's wing is reinforced by interlocking struts, which provide compensating rigidity.*

assist the fliers, but benefit the divers with sturdy breasts that are able to withstand the pressures of the deep. Running prominently down the middle of the sternum is the keel, or carina. This bladelike bone, unique to birds, anchors the large pectoral muscles responsible for lift-off.

Another triangular structure, the wishbone, or furcula, is essentially a pair of fused collarbones that ensure a bird's powerful downstrokes don't crush its rib cage and internal organs. The furcula also stores part of the downstroke energy for release in the return stroke, greatly boosting efficiency. Flightless birds have all but lost the keel, but the furcula persists—to the delight of everyone who has ever made a wish while pulling one apart.

Flying is a complicated affair, requiring phenomenal eyesight and the processing of large amounts of sensory data. Not surprisingly, birds have relatively large eyes and brains. But space is at a premium, so the eyes of most birds are prominently located on either the sides or the front of the head, forcing the brain upward and into the back of the skull, a paper-thin collection of bones fused for stress-resistance.

Flying isn't a bird's only job. Without hands, a bird must rely on its beak to seize prey, build a nest, and perform other tasks *(page 14)*. This requires a more flexible neck than that found in mammals. A single ball joint at the intersection of the spine and skull provides the necessary freedom of movement.

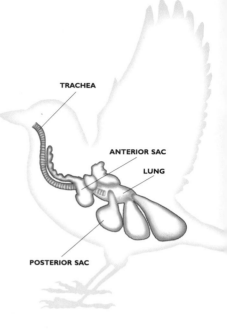

The Respiratory System
The avian respiratory system features a series of air sacs connected to the lungs that permit maximum oxygen absorption during both inhalation and exhalation. The sacs also serve as a cooling system for birds, counteracting the heat generated by their high metabolism.

RESPIRATORY SYSTEM

Although the skeletal structure of birds provides the necessary framework to sustain flight, their internal workings allow birds to produce enough energy to stay in the air. While birds have much smaller lungs than most other vertebrates, the avian respiratory system is, in fact, a model of efficiency.

Birds have evolved an air storage system in the form of a series of air sacs that are attached to the lungs and extend throughout the body cavity—in some cases, even into the bones and tissues. These air sacs serve as temporary storehouses for large amounts of air, enabling birds to take in huge quantities of oxygen—a prerequisite for the demands of flight.

Whereas humans breathe in and out in a simple cycle of inhalation and exhalation, birds have developed a one-way, two-stage process of moving air through their lungs that provides a much more effective exchange of oxygen and carbon dioxide. With a bird's first breath, inhaled air flows into the posterior air sacs. As the bird exhales, this air moves from the sacs into the lungs. With the second inhalation, the oxygen-depleted air is forced from the lung into the anterior air sacs. Finally, with the second exhalation, the originally inhaled air exits the body through the trachea. The result is a continual flow of air through the bird's lungs.

People once thought that birds' breathing and the beating of their wings were synchronized, but the two, in fact, work independently. When they are at rest, birds breathe more slowly than do mammals. But once they have taken to the air, birds can speed up their breathing by as much as twenty times their normal resting rate.

CIRCULATORY SYSTEM

The need to supply large quantities of oxygen and nutrients to the flight muscles demands an equally efficient heart and vascular system. Like the human heart, the center of a bird's circulatory network is a two-pump system that handles venous blood, carrying carbon dioxide and oxygen-rich arterial blood. Although the pump designs are basically similar, a bird's heart is 50 to 100 percent larger and stronger than that of a similarly sized mammal—and for good reason. The resting heart rate of a sparrow, for example, is more than five hundred beats per minute— some seven times the human rate. In cold weather, the heart rate increases to maintain the bird's normal body temperature, which ranges from 100 to 108°F.

BLOOD-FLOW
DIRECTION

KIDNEY

LUNG

HEART

LIVER

The Circulatory System
The circulatory system of a bird takes oxygen-rich blood (red) to the body extremities and returns blood saturated with carbon dioxide (blue) to the heart in an endless loop.

Feet of Engineering

From the powerful talons of an osprey to the flexible webs of a loon, bird feet serve as a reminder that for every need in nature there is a solution; for every niche, a foot perfectly adapted to its environment. Ostriches, for example, have incredibly strong toes, though only two, designed for striding quickly over ground, while the curved claws of a great horned owl clamp like pincers under the weight of its prey, sinking ever more deeply into the flesh of its victim.

Specialized adaptations enable birds to keep their footing no matter what the situation—or weather. Ptarmigan toes develop a dense layer of feathers in winter: nature's own snowshoes. The long spidery toes of the jacana distribute the bird's weight evenly over lily pads floating on the surface of a pond.

Toasty Toes

A thick coat of down and feathers protects a bird's body from the bitter cold of winter. But how do its exposed legs and feet endure such inhospitable weather conditions? The secret lies in a specialized circulatory system that constricts blood flow to the feet by up to 90 percent. In a bird's legs, arteries supplying warm blood to the feet intertwine with veins carrying the blood back again. Heat is transferred to the returning blood both to keep it from freezing and to prevent it from reducing the core temperature of the bird's sensitive major organs.

While birds are often on the move, their feet at times must serve to help them stay put. Perching birds sit securely on a telephone wire or tree branch—even when sound asleep—thanks to an ingenious mechanism that locks their toes in place. As the bird bends its legs to crouch on its perch, tendons attached to the toes pull back around the bent joints, forcing the toes to close. Grooves on the tendons and the sheath surrounding them act like a ratchet to keep the tendons from slipping.

Coming in for a kill, an osprey extends its death-dealing talons toward its prey.

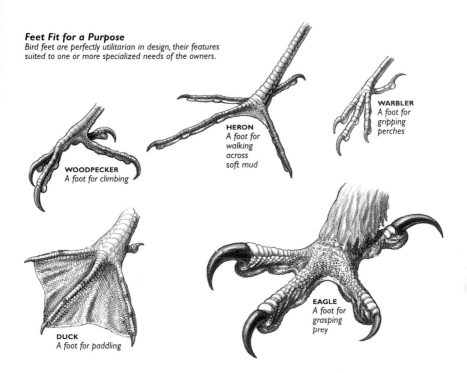

Feet Fit for a Purpose
Bird feet are perfectly utilitarian in design, their features suited to one or more specialized needs of the owners.

WOODPECKER
A foot for climbing

HERON
A foot for walking across soft mud

WARBLER
A foot for gripping perches

DUCK
A foot for paddling

EAGLE
A foot for grasping prey

LEGS OF EVERY LENGTH

In a crouched position, a bird appears to have knees that bend backward, but what look like knees are actually the anatomical equivalent of human ankles—the true knees lie hidden higher up on the legs, beneath the feathers. These pairs of joints divide the legs of all birds into three sections. Leg lengths, however, range from the very long and delicate stilts of wading birds such as egrets to the tiny, weak stubs of swifts—birds that rarely land.

The adaptations are almost limitless. The legs of swimming birds are specially developed for life in the water. Duck legs are attached far back on the body to provide the most efficient propulsion—a design that also accounts for the bird's waddling gait on land. Grebes' legs are actually flattened to provide as little resistance as possible when the birds move through the water.

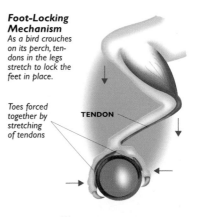

Foot-Locking Mechanism
As a bird crouches on its perch, tendons in the legs stretch to lock the feet in place.

Toes forced together by stretching of tendons

TENDON

A Beak for Every Need

Nutcracker, spear, sieve, pry bar, preening tool, tweezers, insect net, filter, awl: Birds' beaks serve an impressive array of roles—on land, in the air, and under water.

There is a purpose for every beak, no matter how curious the design. The black skimmer, for example, has a lower bill longer than the upper. This ungainly look-ing design allows the bird to slice through the water with the lower mandible while it flies just above the surface, snaring crustaceans and fish as it goes. The avocet, on the other hand, has an upward-curved bill that can pluck tiny shrimp from shallow water as the beak is swept from side to side, while the delicate

beak of a hummingbird often matches the size and shape of the hummer's preferred flower.

A beak is adapted not only to what a bird eats, but also to how it tracks down its meal. Pileated woodpeckers and whip-poor-wills both dine on insects. But the wood-pecker has a sturdy, daggerlike beak for drilling into tree bark like a tiny jackhammer, while the whip-poor-will, a somewhat lazier hunter, has virtually no beak at all—it simply cruises through the air with its mouth open wide, waiting for din-ner to fly in.

One of the best examples of beaks at work can be seen at the backyard feeder, where a carpet of husks

A Collection of Beaks
Beaks come in many shapes and sizes, each suited to a bird's particular diet and food-tracking methods.

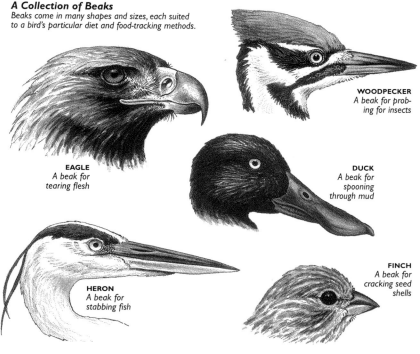

WOODPECKER
A beak for prob-ing for insects

EAGLE
A beak for tearing flesh

DUCK
A beak for spooning through mud

HERON
A beak for stabbing fish

FINCH
A beak for cracking seed shells

Unlike most birds, the flamingo possesses a large lower bill and a smaller upper one. This design is perfect for the novel way a flamingo feeds—with its head upside down.

beak to take a beating without rattling the bird's brain. Woodpeckers benefit from a layer of cerebral–spinal fluid that cushions the blows of their industrious hammering.

The bills themselves are lightweight bony structures covered by a tough sheathing of keratin—the same material that makes up the nails of humans. But unlike nails, the bills are loaded with cells and receptors that make them as sensitive to touch *(page 28)* as human lips and fingertips. The snipe, for example, can stick its bill into the ground and sense the movement of a worm boring nearby.

The cells are continually replaced as they are destroyed or worn away by activities of the bird. And there are reports that the beaks of some species, such as storks, can even be regenerated after they have been severely damaged.

on the ground serves as a testament to the dexterity and strength of beaks in shelling seeds. Some finches use their tongues to hold seeds against horny ridges on the roofs of their mouths. Moving their bottom bills forward and back in a sawing motion, they slit the husks open. Other finches crunch seeds, their beaks generating a hundred pounds of pressure—no mean feat for birds that weigh only a few ounces.

THE STRUCTURE OF BEAKS

Unlike the jaws of mammals, birds' beaks consist of upper and lower mandibles that are both hinged, allowing birds to snap their beaks closed quickly and precisely. Each mandible is attached to the skull separately with a series of shock-absorbing joints that permit the

Darwin's Finches

On his expedition to the Galapagos Islands in 1835, Charles Darwin noted that the beaks of various finches were shaped differently. Years later he realized these beaks were yet more proof that a species evolves to take advantage of a niche. The beaks of Darwin's finches, as the birds are now known, include conical bills for crunching seeds and longer, pointed bills for feeding on cactus flowers.

The Digestive Tract

With their high metabolic rates, birds demand a digestive system that quickly converts food into energy. The process begins with the beak, a remarkable organ that selects and manipulates food *(page 14)*. The mouth and tongue are outfitted with comblike fibers, called

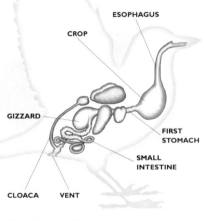

ESOPHAGUS

CROP

GIZZARD

FIRST STOMACH

SMALL INTESTINE

CLOACA   **VENT**

The Digestive Tract
Easily digested food such as fruit can pass through a bird's digestive system in fifteen minutes; seeds and nuts may take several hours.

papillae, that move food along like a down escalator. Three salivary glands lubricate the mouth, easing the transport of food.

Having eliminated teeth during the evolutionary process for weight considerations, birds rely on strong chemicals to process their food. The esophagus, or gullet, emits these potent digestive juices. In some species, such as the pigeon, the fluid is chemically similar to human breast milk and also is fed to the young. Pigeons, sage grouse, and other species have found an additional

external use for the esophagus as well, inflating it grandiloquently in courtship displays.

In some cases, the digestive system can't keep up with the pace of eating, particularly among seed eaters and leaf eaters such as grouse and pheasants. Assistance for these fast eaters comes in the form of a pouchlike crop, where food is stored until it can be digested later.

Birds have two stomachs, which perform different tasks in different species. Some birds use them selectively, storing one kind of food, nectar, for instance, while diverting another, such as insects, for full digestion. The first stomach, or proventriculus, is a gland that breaks down food with chemical enzymes, which in fish eaters and birds that swallow animals whole are powerful enough to dissolve the bones of prey. The second stomach is known to science as the ventriculus, but more often goes by its jaunty popular name, the gizzard. It acts as the "teeth" of the bird, and is an elaborate grinding muscle. Supplied with ample roughage such as quartz grit, it actually could turn steel needles and walnut shells to mush.

From the gizzard, food passes into the small intestine. "Small" is a relative term here; the intestine of a swift is three times the bird's body length, but in an ostrich it is more than twenty times the length. Generally, fruit and meat eaters have shorter intestines, while the rough diet of seed and insect eaters

A bird's double-stomach digestive process helps it not only fuel itself but, in some cases, also feed its offspring. This brown pelican has regurgitated its partially digested meal to feed its chick.

requires a longer apparatus. The bulk of digestion takes place here, through the action of enzymes and bile injected by the pancreas and liver. The food, broken down into its chemical parts, is absorbed through the intestinal walls.

Finally, waste materials are strained before leaving the body through the cloaca, which joins the digestive, urinary, and reproductive tracts. Here water is reabsorbed from urine and waste solidifies for excretion from the vent.

The efficiency of the avian digestive tract varies with food type. The hummingbird, for example, can convert up to 99 percent of the nectar it consumes into energy, while the spruce grouse, a leaf eater, manages only 30 percent. In general, carnivores assimilate food energy more efficiently than herbivores. All of them transform it into glucose, a source of quickly available power.

The Role of Pellets

Whatever the gizzard can't assimilate as food is either passed on as waste or regurgitated in the form of pellets. Pellets consist of anything and everything—from insect exoskeletons and crustacean shells to teeth, bones, and dirt, as well as accidentally ingested objects. Birds of prey, which may ingest fur and bone, must regurgitate pellets between meals. This is especially critical for the owls, which swallow prey whole. More than three hundred bird species are known to pass pellets.

Bird Brains

Sprinkling bits of leaves on the water, a green heron waits patiently to snap up the fish that come to investigate the bait. Traditionally, ornithologists believed that bird behavior was ruled almost entirely by instinct. But the actions of birds such as the heron seem to point to a real spark of intelligence in those bird brains. And while much of birds' complex behavior does depend on instinct, evidence suggests that it can be modified by learning and experience.

IN THE WILD

Adaptation of wild birds to their human neighbors offers fascinating examples of spontaneous inventiveness. When door-to-door milk delivery began in England, titmice soon learned to pick through the foil bottle caps to reach the cream underneath. Although these birds may be preprogrammed to peck at objects to get at their food, the knowledge that milk bottles offered a source of food must have been learned.

Members of the corvid family, such as crows, are often favored as the most intelligent birds. Hooded crows in Norway, for example, will steal fish and bait from an angler's line in winter by pulling the line out of the hole in the ice and walking toward the hole, keeping their feet on the line to stop it from slipping. The fact that such birds as crows have a varied diet and collect their food in a number of different ways may be attributed to a mental flexibility in the family of birds that puts others to shame. However, many of their most clever achievements clearly point to individual bird ingenuity at work.

IN THE LAB

In many laboratory intelligence tests, birds outperform small mammals.

Some clever birds in the wild use tools to get at their food. This woodpecker finch, lacking the long beak of a real woodpecker, relies on a cactus spine to get the job done.

Pigeons in the lab have been taught to move a box under a dangling banana to reach the food, and some studies claim that pigeons can be taught to count to seven.

Some of the most interesting laboratory studies show how the natural behavior of birds can be modified by experience. In one UCLA experiment, male village weavers raised in isolation were able to construct the same kind of intricately designed nests as their wild cousins. As the seasons went by, the researchers observed that the weavers became even more adept nest builders, proving that practice does, indeed, make perfect.

Other studies focus on how birds profit by observing. Scientists at Germany's University of Ruhr investigated the instinct of blackbirds to mob predators that threaten their nests. Experimenters placed pairs of blackbirds in facing cages. One of each pair was shown a stuffed owl, its natural predator, while the other was shown a harmless honeycreeper. The blackbird that saw the owl emitted a warning call and tried to attack it. The other bird responded by trying to attack the honeycreeper it saw. After a few repetitions of this lesson, the second blackbird learned to mob the honeycreeper whenever it was presented. Although blackbirds may be born with an instinct that drives them to mob a predator, birds apparently can learn—even

Alex, the Celebrity Parrot

Ask a bird what it knows and few will be able to answer. But Alex, an African gray parrot raised by researcher Irene Pepperberg, can do exactly that. The University of Arizona scientist has taught Alex

to distinguish among fifty objects by name—from keys to paper— and to categorize these objects in abstract ways. Presented with an object, Alex can respond to the questions, "What color?" "Green." "What shape?" "Three corner" (triangle). When presented with one red and one green plastic key and asked, "What's different?" he will respond, "Color."

incorrectly, as in the case of the experiment with the honeycreeper—which birds pose a threat to them.

INSIDE THE SKULL

The anatomy of birds' brains themselves was once thought to support the idea that birds are mere slaves of instinct. The cerebral cortex, the outer layer of the brain that governs learned behaviors in mammals, is underdeveloped in birds and can in fact be completely removed without significantly affecting the behavior of the birds. However, further research suggests that birds possess well-developed circuits within their brains, which may account for their ability to learn.

Focus on Eyes

Eagle-eyed isn't a misnomer: Eagles and other raptors possess keener eyesight than humans.

A hawk swoops down on a small bird darting through a dense forest canopy to elude capture. The drama is a test for the sophisticated vision of both birds. The powers of avian eyesight are legendary, and growing scientific knowledge of how birds' visual acumen functions has only increased our respect.

Whether hunting, communicating, migrating, or just plain flying, a bird must gather and process an incredible amount of information almost instantaneously while airborne. This seemingly daunting task is handled easily by the sharpest eyes in the animal world. Good eyes are every bit as essential to flight as good wings.

Sharp-Eyed Wonders

Powerful sight is a product of many factors. In birds, it begins with the shape of the eye. The hawk's eye is relatively round, but it features a flattened lens far from the retina, the receiving end of light. This gives hawks what photographers would call a long focal length, like a telephoto lens. The field of vision is narrower than that attained by the flatter eye shape that most birds have, but the smaller image is projected onto more optical cells, resulting in a larger image that provides better resolution. In addition, the retinal wall of the hawk contains more than 1 million cones per square millimeter—more than three times the number in a human eye. As in a camera, there are trade-offs to a long focal length. Usually, the image is darker, and "slower" because not as much light is admitted to the eye. The hawk overcomes this potential handicap through a large pupil that floods the eye with light.

All birds have a fovea, a region of higher resolution that gives a sharper image. Hawks and other raptors have two—one that offers good depth perception for nearby objects, and the other for looking at a distance.

Equipped with this advanced visual system, the hawk occupies a special niche atop the avian food chain.

Birds' eyes are large and prominent. In humans, the eyes make up 1 percent of total head weight; in birds, they may represent up to 15 percent. The lens and cornea bubble outward at an angle, held in place by a ring of a dozen small, flat bones. The eyes take up all available space where they are anchored—in some birds nearly touching one another—and push the brain up and to the rear of the skull.

A VISION FOR DIFFERENT NICHES

Eye placement in birds is determined by the behavior and ecological niche of the particular species. The eyes of predators face forward, giving these birds a high degree of binocular vision that makes it easier for them to pick out prey from solid backgrounds. The eyes of prey species, on the other hand, are located laterally for best sighting of onrushing predators. This monocular vision provides a wide field of vision, but not stereoscopic depth perception. Still, it is useful.

Certain birds have additional adaptations to improve their vision. Goatsuckers, cuckoos, and other species can even look backward just by flexing certain muscles. Pigeons can rotate their heads, giving them some three hundred degrees of vision. The bittern has another solution. It freezes with its bill in the air like a reed when predators are near; low-mounted eyes allow it to keep a lookout beneath its head.

The avian eye itself is similar to what other vertebrates possess, with a cornea, lens, iris, and retina separated by a gelatinous mass called the vitreous humor. But there are important differences that make birds' eyes beautifully adapted to their lifestyle and ecological niche. They are flatter, giving birds a larger image in focus at any one time. And focusing is more effective in birds because both cornea and lens may be bent to hone in on a subject. In human eyes, only the lenses change shape.

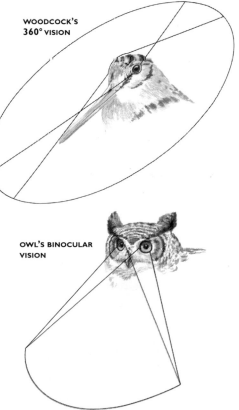

WOODCOCK'S 360° VISION

OWL'S BINOCULAR VISION

Visual Fields
Eye placement affects how a bird sees. The woodcock has eyes mounted far back on its head, allowing it to see predators both behind and ahead. The eyes of the owl are situated up front, providing keen binocular vision that assists it in spotting prey.

The most important distinction lies in the retina, the concave rear wall of the eye. The avian retina is twice as thick as that of other vertebrates, and is marked by one or two foveae—areas of a greater density of photo receptors and retinal nerve cells that sharpen image resolution. Humans and other vertebrates have only one fovea. This zone of maximum sharpness is used for inspecting the fine detail of objects when needed and for fixing on predators and prey. When some birds need additional information about depth, they bob their heads, allowing them to better gauge distance by comparing how objects that are close at hand appear to move more quickly than those that are far way.

Birds' eyes also have a strange ribbed structure made of blood vessels, known as the pecten. Well developed in birds, the pecten is a mysterious organ that protrudes into the vitreous humor, where the optic nerve bundle joins the retina. There are dozens of theories to explain its function, ranging from glare reduction to thermostat. The pecten most likely provides additional nutrients to the retina.

A Bird's Eye
Except for the pecten, the role of which is still debated by biologists, a bird's eye has many of the basic features found in the human eye. Most birds have one fovea, the point of sharpest vision, which looks outward at right angles to the body; some birds, such as hawks and eagles, also have a second fovea, located in the corner of the eye, which looks forward toward the beak.

RETINA
VITREOUS HUMOR
LENS
FOVEA
PECTEN
CORNEA
OPTIC NERVE

RODS AND CONES

A bird's retina contains more of the critical optical cells, known as cones and rods, in its tissues than other vertebrates. Cone cells are responsible for color and sharpness, allowing a hummingbird to spot a flower at a distance of half a mile.

House sparrows have more than ten times as many cone cells as humans. Rod cells enable vision in low light. Most nocturnal birds possess more rods than cones, and thus have poor color vision.

Not only are there more optic cells in a bird's eye than in a human's, but there are more fibers in each nerve connecting these cells to the brain. A pigeon boasts nearly two-and-a-half times as many nerve fibers as a human. Birds bolster this superiority with almost ten thousand efferent, or centrifugal, nerve fibers leading from the brain back to the eye. These seem to provide constant stimulation to the retinal cells.

Everything about birds—from their specialized eating habits to their gender coloration—suggests that they have advanced color vision. The number and nature of cone cells prove it. Each cone cell contains a

Nictitating membranes, or third eyelids, play a variety of roles in birds, from moisteners and cleaners to protective shields.

droplet of colored oil—red, orange, yellow, or green. The exact mechanism of color vision in birds is poorly understood, but most likely the oils function like lens filters on a camera, providing heightened color contrast. Red and yellow drops in the eyes of pigeons may filter green and blue light from the ground and the sky, making predators easier to spot, while red droplets in a kingfisher's eyes may reduce glare off water, allowing it to see fish swimming below the surface.

Bird vision may extend beyond the range of light visible to the human eye and into the ultraviolet (UV) wavelength. This affects not only how a bird sees, but its social life as well. In one experiment, scientists reduced the ability of the throat plumage of male bluethroats, a European songbird, to reflect UV light. The birds sang less and had less success in attracting mates.

A THIRD EYELID

Protecting the eyes of birds are pairs of lids; but each eye also has a third lid, the nictitating membrane, a relic of which lies in the inner corner of the human eye. The membranes are sheer curtains of skin that serve birds in many ways. Containing tiny brushlike cells, they clean and moisten the corneas with each blink. Some diving birds use the membranes as contact lenses to improve their vision, while owls use them as shutters and magpies as billboards, displaying large orange spots. When they sleep, birds close the outermost lids, setting up opaque barriers to a world they see almost too well.

Window Warnings

Birds often are unable to distinguish the real thing from its reflection in a sliding glass door or kitchen window. You can help by hanging strips of plastic or tin foil or even chimes in front of the glass. Another option is to apply window stickers.

Hearing

The bubbling, melodious notes of a bluebird may delight our ears, but of course humans are not the intended audience. Does the bird's mate perched in a neighboring tree hear what we do?

The answer is yes—but with some interesting exceptions. Humans and most bird species can best hear sounds with a frequency of between 1 and 5 kHz (thousand cycles per second), although there

birds seldom hear sounds above 12 kHz; humans, in contrast, hear sounds of up to 20 kHz.

Some researchers believe that songbirds may surpass humans in an area known as temporal resolution—the ability to distinguish individual sounds in a very rapid-fire sequence, which human ears would tend to hear as blended together. In other words, while people may enjoy the beauty of

Oilbirds, which nest in dark caves, rely on echolocation to navigate.

are reports of birds detecting frequencies as low as 1 cycle per second. During World War I, observers noted that birds in French aviaries reacted to noise from battles being waged many miles away, beyond the range detectable by humans. Thunder, too, is picked up by birds at great distances. These infrasounds travel particularly well through the atmosphere, enabling birds to hear them at astounding distances. But

birds' conversation, they may be missing some of the exact wording.

Just as the beaks and feet of birds are designed for the demands of a particular niche, so, too, does their hearing vary according to needs. Owls can perceive exceptionally faint sounds, allowing them to pick up on the scurrying of mice far below. One researcher at Queen's University in Kingston, Ontario, discovered that the owl he was studying would react to the sound of two fingers gently rubbed together up to a yard away. And baby chicks are attuned to respond to the low-frequency clucks of their mothers.

Oilbirds, a species of South America, rely on hearing to help them fly. The birds emit a very rapid series of clicks and use the deflection of the sounds off cave walls to navigate and to find their own nests—a process of echolocation similar to that used by bats to navigate in the dark.

While some birds rely on hearing to detect their prey, others exploit weaknesses in a predator's hearing to escape detection. All birds use the difference in volume and timing of sounds arriving at each ear to locate a sound's source. But at certain volumes and frequencies, this system breaks down. Some songbirds' distress calls occur exactly in a predator's "weak spot." So, while a hawk may hear the call, it can't tell from which direction the sound is coming.

INSIDE THE EAR

The anatomy of birds' ears is similar to that of mammals. The external and middle cavities of the ear collect sound and funnel it to the inner ear. Receptors in the cochlea, a curved, fluid-filled organ of the inner ear, register the sound and transmit it to the brain. As in mammals, the inner ear also plays a role in the maintaining of balance.

Although the inside workings of birds' ears are much the same as those of mammals, birds' ears lack

An Asymmetrical Advantage

An owl swoops out of the blackness and snares a mouse with its talons. How? Infrared vision? A sixth sense? Actually, this uncanny ability stems from a curious ear arrangement. The right ear of a barn owl is higher than the left and also directed slightly upward, making it more sensitive to sounds from above the horizontal; the left ear is angled downward, attuned to sounds from below the horizontal. In saw-whet owls, the asymmetry carries through to the skull design *(below)*. The asymmetry allows owls to pinpoint sound sources both horizontally and vertically with unmatched accuracy. Lab tests show that barn and saw-whet owls can zero in on a sound vertically with an accuracy of from one to three degrees—the width roughly of a finger held at arm's length.

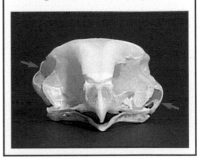

mammals' ears prominent exterior structure. Birds do, though, have external muscular rims around their ears. Special feathers attached to these rims flatten against the ear openings, blocking out gusts of air during flight while still allowing sound to enter. Some diving birds can seal their ears completely with feathers, protecting them from damage caused by changes in pressure they experience underwater.

Smell and Taste

Birds aren't gourmands. They don't swoon at the aroma or sing about the taste of expertly prepared meals. This is because the parts of their brains that process smell—the olfactory lobes—are small. Birds also boast relatively few tastebuds: A quail possesses a total of sixty-two, while a human may have as many as nine thousand.

Nonetheless, the senses of smell and taste are important in bird behavior. The sense of smell is best developed in birds that nest alone or in colonies on the ground, in carnivores, and in birds that live near water. Tests with one species of storm petrel demonstrate that the birds find their way home by smell; the coastal dwellers descend from the sky into their home forest and proceed upwind to their burrows. Pigeons apparently also navigate by smell when near their lofts. Smell is not a well-developed sense in most perching birds, in pelicans, and in herbivores, perhaps because they don't need to rely on it as much to survive.

The olfactory structure itself is another gem of efficiency in a small space. Birds inhale through nostrils usually located at the base of their bills. In some diving birds, the nasal openings are shielded by thin flaps, or operculums. Hummingbirds bear the flaps as well, employing them to prevent the inhalation of clogging

Turkey vultures' sense of smell is so keen that they were once used to find leaks in a forty-two-mile long gas pipe. Engineers put ethyl mercaptan (the odorous substance in carrion) in the pipe and found the leaks where the birds circled.

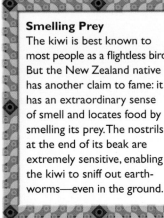

Smelling Prey

The kiwi is best known to most people as a flightless bird. But the New Zealand native has another claim to fame: it has an extraordinary sense of smell and locates food by smelling its prey. The nostrils at the end of its beak are extremely sensitive, enabling the kiwi to sniff out earthworms—even in the ground.

pollens while they have their beaks buried deep in flowers.

Air passes through the nostrils into three irregularly shaped chambers. The walls of all three of these chambers contain many folds, or conchae. The resulting rippled complexity creates an increased contact surface for air, allowing it to be cleaned and scanned for odor. The first chamber is rich in blood vessels, while the middle chamber is a conchae-filled scroll lined with sensory cells. Together, the first two chambers heat, scrub, and humidify inhaled air.

The third chamber contains olfactory receptor cells with hairlike nerves that reach all the way to the lining of the nasal wall. The third chamber smells air inhaled from the nostrils. The receptor cells of the third chamber receive the scent of food as it drifts along a passage connecting the chamber to the mouth. This important mechanism enables birds to make sure that what they are eating isn't spoiled or diseased.

Birds use taste to perform the same crucial task. Their taste buds are generally located right up front, in the mucous membrane of the mouth near the salivary glands, either on the tongue or jaw, though mallards concentrate theirs at the tip of the bill.

Despite the modest size of the bird's taste mechanism, it is nonetheless effective. Sanderlings, for example, can differentiate between sand samples that contain worms and those that don't merely by taste. Bitterness doesn't seem to be a problem for many birds, which tolerate formic acid in their diet of ants and other insects. But parrots shy away from salt in even low concentrations. Whether by smell or taste, birds clearly know what they like and what they don't.

WRYNECK

BANANAQUIT

SHEARWATER

RED-BREASTED MERGANSER

An Array of Tongues
What they lack in number of tastebuds, bird tongues make up in variety of shapes. Some tastebuds are also located on the palate.

WHITE-HEADED WOODPECKER

2 7

Touch

Ducks, such as these mallards, rely on the touch receptors in their beaks to probe for food under water where it may be impossible to see.

With their sharp claws, hard beaks, and dinosaur ancestry, birds seem unlikely to be sensitive to tactile stimulation. For one thing, few places on a bird's body are exposed to the elements; feathers almost completely envelop it. And yet birds are quite "touchy feely," even if not in ways we might expect.

Special touch receptors—bunlike sensory cells that encase an interior filled with nerve fibers—are located in key areas of the body, primed to shoot signals to the brain. Their placement depends on where they can do the most good and that depends, in turn, on the species' behavior. One type, which resembles the human touch receptors, is found in the woodpecker's tongue

and the duck's beak, where sensitive touch is essential to careful, accurate feeding. Woodpeckers, for example, can place their bills in freshly bored holes and feel vibrations of bugs nearby. They use that information to help them locate exactly where to drill their next holes.

Other species that depend on their beaks for finding food—snipes, sandpipers, and other shorebirds, for example—also have bundles or sacs of receptors in the tips of their bills. In these birds, the beak acts as a seismograph, registering the slightest under-ground or underwater movement of a worm, crustacean, or fish.

Conveniently, the bill can also snag whatever it happens to find—

and quickly. The wood stork's snare has been timed at less than two one-hundredths of a second, twice as fast as the length of time it takes a human to blink at a firecracker.

Birds also need a highly tuned sense of touch in order to fly. Reacting to changing air currents, darting through foliage, and alighting on fence posts, they must constantly adjust to their environment. Touch provides information that even their superb eyesight can't deliver. Highly sensitive touch receptors have been found in the follicles of wing feathers, where they can detect the most transient external change and trigger an immediate physical response.

Some scientists speculate that these cells of birds may also be sensitive to very low-frequency vibrations, since sacs of receptors located between the upper and lower legs have been found to process low-frequency impulses. The cells might even respond to other movements within the bird's body, such as in the muscles.

If all this is true, then flying is much more than flapping and gliding, instead the result of a perfectly tuned system that works with a constant loop of information feedback directing virtually all body parts and the brain.

The bill of this western sandpiper (above) is loaded with touch receptors that provide information about its probing activities. The oystercatcher (below) depends mainly on its vision to locate shells. Not surprisingly, its touch receptors are not as well developed as those of the sandpiper.

THE MIRACLE OF FLIGHT

From a hawk riding a thermal high into the sky to a humming-bird hovering seemingly motionless in the air, bird flight symbolizes freedom and mobility. The miracle is that it happens at all.

Birds make flying look easy—so easy that the full marvel of the accomplishment isn't readily apparent. Here, after all, is a group of animals that seems to defy gravity, one of Earth's fundamental forces. Birds were the models for airplanes, but their flight systems put these ponderous human machines to shame. For efficiency, control, and elegance, nothing can match a bird's mastery of the air.

It all begins with the ingenious shape of the wing: a simple airfoil. An airfoil is a curved plane with a leading edge thicker than its trailing edge. Flight is possible because the top surface is more strongly curved than the bottom, which makes the top surface longer.

It happens this way: As the leading edge moves forward, it splits the air into two currents. The top current has farther to travel and speeds up to meet the bottom current at the rear of the wing. The faster the air moves across the top of the wing, the more the air pressure there is reduced. The combination of the higher pressure beneath the airfoil-wing and the lower pressure above literally pushes the whole surface upward.

Of course, in order for this effect to result in flight, birds must generate some kind of forward motion: They must take off. Some birds, such as gulls, can simply extend their

"Higher still and higher
From the earth
thou springest
Like a cloud of fire"

— PERCY BYSSHE SHELLEY
"To a Skylark "

With its legs dangling behind and its neck curved into a distinctive S-shape, a great egret flies effortlessly over its watery habitat.

On the downstroke, the power stroke, the primary feathers on the outer section of the wings are twisted at an angle and bite into the air, acting as propellers. On the upstroke, the primaries open to let air pass freely through them, making the wings easier to lift.

wings, push off with their feet into a roaring wind, and achieve the necessary lift. Others, such as coots and other waterfowl, need long runways and furious flapping to generate enough speed to fly. Still others with large wingspans, such as gannets, dive from cliffs or other precipices, free-falling until there is sufficient wind passing over their wings to support them.

Like an airplane, a flying bird has to contend with two main aerodynamic forces: lift and drag. But unlike an airplane, a bird has wings with two functional parts: an inner part, nearest the body, moved by the shoulder joint; and an outer part,

controlled separately by the bird's "wrist." Acting as a propeller, this outer section of each wing, with its complement of primary flight feathers—or primaries—exerts downward and backward pressure as it pushes the bird along in flapping flight. Meanwhile, the inner part of each wing, with its secondary feathers, provides the bird with the necessary lift by tilting slightly upward and forward, just like the flaps on an airplane's wing.

Anatomy of an Airfoil
Air rushing over the upper surface of an airfoil must travel farther than the air passing underneath, causing it to speed up. The resulting drop in air pressure provides lift that helps overcome the force of gravity.

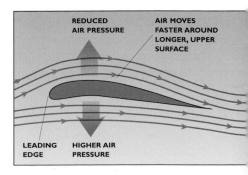

REDUCED AIR PRESSURE

AIR MOVES FASTER AROUND LONGER, UPPER SURFACE

LEADING EDGE

HIGHER AIR PRESSURE

Diving waterfowl, such as this red-throated loon, tend to have small wings in relation to their body weight. This makes it more difficult for them to take off. Such birds frequently require a long runway and furious running along the water before they become airborne—typically at a speed of twenty miles per hour.

minute alterations in wing shape and orientation. Lift depends on a certain velocity of air passing across the wings and the flow can be maintained only when the inclination of the wings—the angle of attack—is relatively shallow. When the angle becomes too steep relative to the bird's speed, turbulence develops, interrupting the airflow across the top of the wings. This is called a stall. Lift disappears and the bird falls. Birds use more than fifty separate wing muscles to stay aloft and many of these help shift feathers to create slots in the wings. The slots regulate air flow and prevent—or exploit— the tendency to stall.

During free flight, two opposing powerful pectoral muscles move each whole wing up and down from the shoulder. Powered by the contracting pectoralis muscles, the wings sweep through the downstroke fully extended. At the end of the downstroke, these muscles relax and another large breast muscle, the supracoracoideus, contracts and pulls the wings upward. On the upstroke, the primary feathers near the ends of the wings separate slightly like louvres to allow air through, reducing resistance as the wings move up and back against the air. Although the primaries twist slightly to provide a small amount of thrust on the upstroke, the overwhelming force of propulsion comes from the downstroke.

THE ANGLE OF ATTACK

Proper wing position is essential for flight, especially at take-off and landing. Birds maneuver by making

Flightless Birds

Flying is an exhausting business— so much so that over the millennia, some types of birds have found they can do without it. Flightless birds come in all sizes and shapes, from tiny wrens to giant ostriches. Some, such as roadrunners, can still fly but spend most of their time on the ground. Far from handicapped, these species actually evolved from flying birds to better exploit ecological niches on the ground or in the water. The wings of penguins, for example, are small and don't fold— perfect for undersea propulsion, but

A great horned owl drops to its perch, slowing its speed to a stall just as it alights.

A bird's landing is essentially a controlled stall. The trick is to slow to a stop without falling. Most birds extend their airfoil surface area by engaging the tail and spreading the primaries near the ends of the wings, increasing the angle of attack while at the same time lowering the tail for added braking power.

Most birds manage to pull up over a landing spot and drop matter-of-factly to the ground. Water birds drop their pudgy webbed feet like landing gear to increase wind resistance and braking. Birds that land on branches or telephone wires need keen eyesight, precision stall control, and firm foot grip.

unsuitable as engines of lift. Propelled by flipperlike wings, the emperor penguin dives into icy Antarctic waters to depths of seven hundred feet and more.

So why did some birds turn their backs on the sky? There are several reasons. Economy of energy, for one. Flying burns up a lot of calories, so flying birds must spend a great deal of time searching for food. Flightless birds don't have the same energy demands and can moderate their eating—an advantage at times of food shortage.

Weight also plays a factor. Flight muscles take up a disproportionate amount of a bird's weight—roughly 15 percent of most birds. There also comes a point when a bird is simply too heavy to fly. The three-hundred-pound ostrich, for example has evolved powerful legs, rather than wings, for avoiding predators.

For all its advantages, flightlessness comes with a price: increased vulnerability. Many species of flightless birds, such as the great auk that once lived in the North Atlantic, have disappeared. Living mostly on islands, many species of flightless birds at one time had no predators. But the arrival of humans exposed their vulnerability and many were hunted to extinction.

Soaring and Hovering

Within the avian world, flying techniques are as varied as the species of birds themselves. The ten-foot-long wingspan of the albatross can harness each ocean breeze like a hang glider and allow miles of soaring without a single flap. On the other end of the spectrum, the tiny hummingbird is a kind of feathered helicopter, able to hover in one spot by means of specially designed wings that whir too fast for the naked eye to see. Every method of flying is dependent on the actual physical characteristics of the bird itself and the habitat in which it lives.

Soaring is a popular technique among birds because it consumes far less energy than flapping wings. But not all soaring is alike. Gliding above land requires a different set of skills than riding the sky above large bodies of water. Inland, birds use thermal soaring to float above the terrain. As the sun beats down and heats the land, columns of warm air rise into the atmosphere. Shifting from updraft to updraft, the most expert soarers are able to read and ride the wind like veteran sailors.

Because water does not warm sufficiently to create these thermal updrafts, seabirds have adopted a different technique, called dynamic soaring, for staying aloft. Whereas thermal soaring finds birds using rising air like an elevator to gain and maintain altitude, dynamic soaring allows birds to exploit the differences in air speed at different levels above the water to achieve the same end.

Flying a hundred feet or so above the waves where the wind blows the strongest, seagulls, petrels, and other seabirds gain air speed; they then swoop down to within inches of the surface, where air speed, reduced by the friction of the waves, is slowest. Wheeling around, the birds use the momentum they gained to fly into the wind, which drives them upward like a kite at the end of a string. High above the water, the birds turn again to ride the wind downward

Two Methods of Soaring
In dynamic soaring (below), seabirds fly effortlessly for hours by taking advantage of the difference in air speed far above the water compared to at its surface, where the air is slowed by waves. In thermal soaring (right), birds such as hawks float upward on rising columns of warm air.

HIGHER
AIR SPEED

SLOWER
AIR SPEED

RISING CURRENTS
OF WARM AIR

Hummingbird Hovering
Mobile shoulder joints enable hummingbirds to generate lift without propulsion throughout both forward stroke and backstroke, as their wings move in a figure-eight pattern (right).

and pick up momentum for the next cycle. This cycle continues for hours or even days on end.

AERIAL ACROBATS

The very antithesis of an eagle hanging in the sky as if suspended by an invisible thread is the dart and blur of the hummingbird. Unlike much larger birds, with wings developed to exploit the varying wind conditions of their environment, hummers rely on their unique physical characteristics to stay aloft.

Hummingbirds do not soar; they hover, suspended seemingly motionless in the air. Their unparalleled ability to fly in the same place is due to an unusual wing and shoulder structure. These remarkable birds possess incredibly flexible shoulders that can pivot almost 180 degrees, enabling them to flap their wings in the shape of a flat figure-eight at up to eighty beats a second. In contrast to other birds, which generate lift on only the forward stroke, the hummer's flapping technique creates continuous lift by pivoting the wings so that the leading edges on the forward stroke remain the leading edges on the backward stroke. This technique requires not only tremendous flexibility but exceptionally strong muscles—30 percent of a hummingbird's weight is taken up by its breast muscles.

Teaching Man to Fly

At least as far back as Icarus, who strapped on wings of wax and soared off—he thought—into the sun, humans have dreamed of flight. One principal stumbling block was the thick-headed insistence that wings had to be flat planes. This could have been easily corrected by examining the wing structure of birds. Astonishingly enough, until the late nineteenth century, few made the connection. Then, the German inventor Otto Lilienthal developed an airfoil, built several prototypes, and, with his brother's help, tested them by leaping off platforms built on hilltops. In the 1890s Lilienthal made a few wobbly sorties and proved the critics of curved wing surfaces wrong.

Starting with the airfoil, other avian traits have been incorporated into human craft. Wing sizes reflect lessons learned from birds: The faster the flying speed, the less area needed to create lift. Like falcons and swifts, jet fighters and high-altitude spy craft have narrow wings. Planes, like birds, tuck away their landing gear during flight to reduce drag, and land by executing a controlled near-stall close to the ground.

F is for Feather

By any measure, feathers are what make a bird a bird. They are the building blocks of avian behavior, serving as flight surfaces, insulators, motion sensors, camouflage, and much more. Feathers make the airborne life possible and birds have a genetic monopoly among living mammals on their production.

A feather begins its life as a humble nub in the epidermis. Soon different layers develop there from epidermal and dermal cells. Spurred on by growth signals from the thyroid and pituitary glands, a feather sprouts within the layers in the form of a mesh of symmetrically coiled roots. Ultimately, the mature feather, anchored in its follicle, bursts through its protective sheath and is preened into place by the bird.

Feathers are made of keratin, a hard substance that contributes to the hair, nails, and scales of other animals. But feather keratin is chemically dissimilar to these other types. It comprises a different combination of amino acids—the result of genetic mutation that long ago set birds on the path to flight. Keratin protects feathers from a world of ills, including abrasion and even deterioration from intense rays of the sun.

Young birds begin to grow feathers almost immediately after birth.

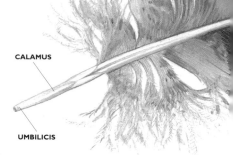

CALAMUS

UMBILICIS

Usually within a matter of weeks—sometimes days—most birds have enough of them to be able to fly. For the rest of the bird's life, feathers are replaced in regular annual molts *(page 44)*.

DIFFERENT TYPES OF FEATHERS
Birds possess an array of feathers, each suited to a particular task. Vaned feathers are the most numerous. They include the contour feathers that gird the body, providing the bird's streamlined shape, and the various flight feathers of the wings and tail. Also known as "typical" feathers, they

A Deadly Obsession
The beauty of bird feathers once proved to be too much of a good thing. In the late 1800s, the habit of bedecking hats with delicate plumes of certain birds took the fashion industry by storm. Birds such as snowy egrets were hunted almost to extinction.
Eventually the campaigns of various concerned conservation groups—and the always-changing fashion trends—put an end to the practice.

SEMIPLUME

DOWN

FILOPLUME

CONTOUR

RACHIS

VANE

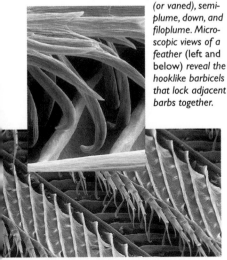

One of nature's great wonders, the feathers of birds come in different forms (above): contour (or vaned), semi-plume, down, and filoplume. Microscopic views of a feather (left and below) reveal the hooklike barbicels that lock adjacent barbs together.

are the defining symbol of avian life and masterpieces of evolution. A vaned feather is built around a hollow quill, or calamus, which is anchored in the skin follicle or, in the case of a flight feather, directly into the bone of the outer wing. The calamus tapers into the rachis, from which the vanes emerge on each side. This is all the naked eye can see, but a closer look, with the help of a microscope, reveals a lattice of barbs and smaller barbules rising diagonally from each vane. The barbules feature tiny hooks called barbicels that lock onto adjacent barbs, weaving the vanes into a dense, tight surface that resists air, water, and cold.

Primary flight feathers, or remiges, line the outer wings. Long

37

The coloring of the flammulated owl's feathers (left) makes it virtually indistinguishable from the tree, while the willow ptarmigan's plumage matches the tundra where it lives.

and stiff, the remiges cut the air and provide propulsion. Secondary flight feathers, which line the inner wings, aid lift and are augmented by vaned "coverts" that handily fill in gaps, completing solid airfoils.

A host of other feathers serve a variety of functions. Short, bushy down feathers lack the hooked barbules, making them less structured. Lying beneath contour feathers, down feathers capture air, insulating the bird from the cold. Semiplumes are even squatter and bushier, and perform a similar function. Filoplumes are small sensitive feathers on long quills that lie among the remiges, often a dozen to a single primary. Linked to the nervous system, they act as flight

data sensors, sending information from the wings to the follicles and on to the brain. Bristles are modified contour feathers. Located around the eyes and nostrils, they filter air and protect these sensitive organs from debris. In some birds, such as whip-poor-wills, they act as whiskers, sensing prey. Finally, powderdown feathers serve an essential but bizarre purpose: They disappear in puffs of powder, depositing a water-repellent coating on the feathers of birds lacking preen or oil glands.

A QUESTION OF CAMOUFLAGE
Flight may be the feather's most important function, but certainly not its only purpose. Penguins rely on dense, streamlined feathers for swimming and insulation. Some species of owl depend on a radial dish of facial feathers to funnel sounds to the ear holes, which are covered by fine feathers just behind the eyes.

Feathers provide both camouflage and communication. Birds

are vulnerable to predators when they are not airborne, and coloration helps them keep a low profile. The ground-dwelling ptarmigan, for example, is a master of disguise. It is white in the winter to blend against snowfields, mottled during the muddy spring, and black and brown during the long, dry mountain summer.

Other birds make use of disruptive shading: bold lines, blotches, or spots break up the outline of the bird's shape. The bands of color across a plover's breast visually separate the head from the body. Still other birds demonstrate counter shading, with a white belly to reflect the color of the ground and a dark back to blend into the surface when sharp-eyed avian predators are on the hunt in the air.

This array of designs is controlled by pigments: melanins, carotenoids, and prophyrins. Melanins are the most important. In addition to providing earth tones, melanins are found in minute granules in a thin layer just below the keratin. These granules not only color, but help strengthen such areas as barbules and wing tips. They also absorb heat and light, enabling birds to regulate body temperature. Carotenoids are responsible for a rainbow of yellows, reds, and blues, and porphyrins control lighter shades of brown and green, and a few exotic colors such as magenta.

Sound-Dampening Feathers

With the constant shifting and adjusting of wing feathers in flight, most birds aren't completely noiseless in the air. This could be a problem for raptors, such as the owl, which hunt at night, since nocturnal rodents and other potential prey have finely honed senses of hearing to compensate for their poor vision. The owl has evolved several key features to allow it to overcome these challenges, and most have to do with feathers. The leading edge of the primary flight feathers feature comblike projections that eliminate noise produced by flapping wings. Normally, overlapping feathers rub across one another as they adjust to changing lift loads, but the owl's wing feathers contain longer barbules that branch off from the barbs. These elongated barbules hold feathers more firmly in place, reducing the need for noisy adjustments in flight. Finally, the wings and body of the owl are lined with velvety feathers that muffle sound. Together, these adaptations make this nocturnal hunter a veritable stealth flier.

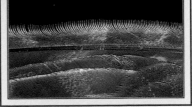

Wings and Tails

In the busy skies above the animal kingdom—complete with bats, buzzing insects, and the occasional flying squirrel—only birds can claim complete air superiority. They owe their success to the design of their wings, which permit flying feats as varied as soaring above a field to dive-bombing toward prey at breakneck speed.

The size and shape of a wing depend on what food the species eats and the type of life the bird lives. Although they vary greatly, wings generally fall into four types. Birds that rely on speed and maneuverability to survive are generally equipped with relatively short elliptical wings, which enable the bird to take off quickly and dart through woods or shrubs in a twisting flight. These are the wings found on most doves, woodpeckers, and perching birds.

High-speed wings tend to be longer and narrower, tapering to a point at the outer tips. The swept-back look resembles a fighter-jet's wings, and indeed the birds that possess these wings can be awesome performers. The peregrine falcon, for instance, can dive toward its prey at speeds of more than 150 miles per hour.

Unlike smaller, aerodynamic birds such as swifts and terns, large species cannot flap their wings for an extended period of time because the action expends too much energy. Instead, many have mastered the art of soaring aloft on air currents. Much like gliding airplanes, these birds possess relatively large wings in relation to their overall weight. The long, broad wings of raptors such as bald eagles and hawks have prominent slots between the feathers where the primaries near the ends of the wings

This gull's wings are similar to those of the albatross— long, narrow, and unslotted, for gliding over water.

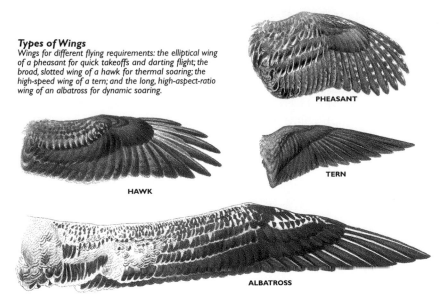

Types of Wings
Wings for different flying requirements: the elliptical wing of a pheasant for quick takeoffs and darting flight; the broad, slotted wing of a hawk for thermal soaring; the high-speed wing of a tern; and the long, high-aspect-ratio wing of an albatross for dynamic soaring.

PHEASANT

HAWK

TERN

ALBATROSS

separate slightly. This makes the wings ideal for soaring upward on rising thermals *(pages 34–35)*.

Oceans gliders, such as gannets and petrels, require a different set of wings—ones with a high-aspect ratio (the ratio of the length of the wing to its width). These seabirds tend to have long, narrow wings, enabling the birds to engage in dynamic soaring over the water *(pages 34–35)*, exploiting the differences in air speed above the waves to fly in endless loops.

THE ROLE OF THE TAIL

Wings contribute the most to bird flight but they don't work alone: the tail also serves as an essential component of the flight gear. Owners of the world's first air brake, birds lower and spread their tail feathers when coming in for a landing. Some birds of prey employ a similar tech-

nique in midair, creating a controlled stall before descending in a final, lightning-quick assault. Birds that need to maneuver quickly, such as pheasants, tend to have longer tails. The stubby-tailed common loon, on the other hand, must take off and land in a straight path.

Tails also play a part in the life of birds when they aren't flying. The long, stiff tail feathers of a woodpecker provide solid support as the bird hammers away at a tree. Similarly, the magpie's lengthy tail is thought to help the bird balance as it hops over ground or perches in trees.

Ironically, the most famous tail in the avian world, belonging to the male peacock, is entirely for show. The ostentatious array of feathers is used to attract mates and intimidate rivals, but the prodigious weight of the display actually makes it difficult for the owner to get airborne.

Preening and Bathing

A goose methodically preening its feathers isn't merely indulging its vanity. Without this essential maintenance, the bird would have difficulty flying or even staying afloat. Feathers that have split lose buoyancy and won't work efficiently in flight. They are also unable to repel water, making it harder for the bird to maintain its body temperature. By gently nibbling at each feather, the bird rearranges separated barbs *(pages 37)*, reconnecting them like the teeth of a zipper.

Preening also serves to re-oil a bird's feathers, keeping them flexible and waterproof, while also helping to fight

fungus and bacteria. The process begins with the bird nudging a special preening gland on its rump with its beak. It then spreads the released oil systematically over its feathers. Of course, not every spot on a bird can be reached with the beak. For areas such as the top of the head, a bird relies on its feet, using them for scratching. Some birds, such as cormorants, even possess a comblike edge on one of their claws to help with the job. Not all birds have preening glands. Some have strange powderdown feathers *(page 38)* to help them with general maintenance.

Others flop down on ant hills or grab the insects and pass them over their feathers. This "anting" is practiced by more than two hundred species. Researchers believe that the formic acid the ants excrete protects birds against fungus and parasites. The practice is so instinctual in some birds that, in the absence of ants, they'll resort to cigarette butts, moth-

A great blue heron takes time out from fishing to preen, spreading oil from its preening gland to its feathers.

Helping Oil-Spill Victims

It's a depressingly familiar sight: sea birds lying on a beach coated with the oily ooze from a tanker spill. The oil does damage in various ways, clogging birds' eyes, ears, and nostrils, and robbing the feathers of their waterproofing and insulating properties, leaving the birds shivering and unable to fly. In a desperate attempt to preen their feathers, many birds die from ingesting the oil. Help sometimes comes from volunteers in the form of repeated baths with mild detergent. Meanwhile, the birds often need to be fed through tubes to keep them alive. While many birds can't survive the shock to their system, some do recover the full use of their feathers and live to return to the wild.

balls, or almost anything else at hand, even though these items are ineffective at the task.

BATHING

Before preening, most birds like a good bath to remove dirt and debris from their feathers. How often birds bathe depends on the weather. Chickadees, for example, bathe up to five times a day in hot weather, taking advantage of birdbaths or small puddles. During cold weather, the same birds may bathe only twice a week.

Just as some humans prefer a quick shower and others a good tub soak, birds have different approaches to bathing. Robins and jays squat in shallow water, ruffling their feathers, rolling from side to side, and flicking their wings to spray water over their backs. Swifts and swallows, which spend most of their time flying, dip quickly into the water from the air, bathing on the wing. Some small birds, such as sparrows, will wet down by flying through damp foliage. Woodpeckers prefer a

shower, standing in the drizzle with wings spread open, while some parrots hang upside down in the rain to get a thorough soaking.

After bathing, birds shake themselves or spread their wings to the sun to dry. Strangely, some species, such as sparrows, follow a bath with a roll in the dirt, forming a hollow in a dusty path and fluttering their wings to coat them with grit. Some ornithologists believe such dust bathing absorbs excess preening oil and protects against lice.

A quick splash in a puddle removes dust from the feathers of a female northern cardinal. Most species bathe before preening.

Molting

No matter how much attention a bird pays to its dress, it sometimes needs a complete change of clothes. A feather can no more be repaired than a fingernail. Eventually, after enough wear and tear, it's time for the bird to molt and acquire new feathers. During molting, worn feathers loosen in their sockets and are pushed out by new feathers growing behind them.

TIMING IS EVERYTHING

Young birds may go through several molting cycles before arriving at their final adult plumage. Once the bird is into adulthood, however, molting generally takes place at a set time of year. It is usually timed so as not to overlap with periods of migration or breeding, possibly because of the energy demands molting puts on the bird. Most songbirds molt in the late summer after the breeding period is over and before migrating starts. Some birds will actually interrupt their molt to migrate. Arctic peregrine

By the time the male summer tanager's molt is complete, the bird will display its all-red finery from beak to tail.

falcons, for example, begin their molt in late summer, but put it on hold until they arrive in the tropics for the winter. Other species will stop in mid-migration to molt.

Many birds change their plumage twice a year, taking advantage of the need to molt to replace a drab winter plumage with a much showier one for the breeding season. In the fall, they switch back to their less gaudy appearance. Winter plumage often includes more feathers for increased insulation. Ptarmigans take advantage of the molt for camouflage purposes, switching from their brown summer feathers to an all-white look for winter.

For some species, the frequency of molting relates to the roughness of their lifestyle. The European

---

Last, but not Least
For some birds, the molting sequence is adapted to their specific needs. While most birds lose their tail feathers from the middle out, many woodpeckers reverse the order to hold onto the middle feathers—used for balancing—for as long as possible.

---

short-toed lark, for example, molts only once a year. But its Asian cousins, which live in deserts where the feathers are subjected to the rigors of sandstorms, molt twice a year. Molting duration also varies from bird to bird. Songbirds usually accomplish the task in less than a month. Perching birds generally take from one to three months to replace all their feathers, while cranes spend a full two years. Some hawks take even longer to completely change their plumage.

MOLTING SEQUENCES

Since molting of all the flight feathers at once would leave birds grounded and helpless, most go through the process gradually, with each species following its own neat sequence. Most songbirds, for example, replace their primary flight feathers beginning at the "wrist joint" and working outward. Rails, however, work in exactly the opposite sequence. Either way, the process must be carefully synchronized between the two wings so the bird can maintain its balance in the air.

Ducks and geese take a different approach entirely. They get their molting over as quickly as possible, losing all their flight feathers at once and replacing them within a couple of weeks. During their flightless period, the birds tend to hide out at secluded lakes where they feel safe. It may be that evolution has favored this approach because ducks and geese are heavy, relative to the surface area of their wings. Since any loss of flight feathers would keep them grounded, they opt for as quick an overhaul as possible.

Theories differ on what triggers molting—hormonal changes following breeding, temperature changes, or changes in the length of the day. The trigger may, in fact, vary from species to species. Even stress plays a factor: Some species have been reported to lose their feathers seemingly from fright.

In winter, a ptarmigan's all-white plumage will blend perfectly into its snowy, Arctic habitat. In summer, the bird molts to acquire the brown feathers that help it hide in the tundra.

THE LIFE OF A BIRD

The life of a bird is usually very brief, and most likely very hard.
It is also a life of simple but immutable cycles.

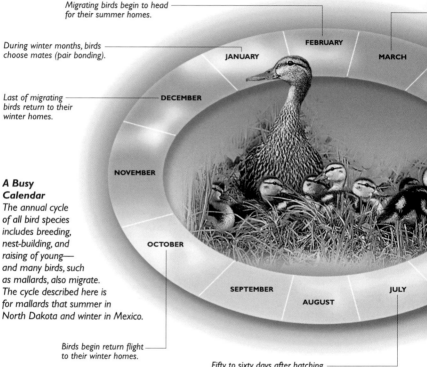

Migrating birds begin to head for their summer homes.

During winter months, birds choose mates (pair bonding).

Last of migrating birds return to their winter homes.

A Busy Calendar
The annual cycle of all bird species includes breeding, nest-building, and raising of young— and many birds, such as mallards, also migrate. The cycle described here is for mallards that summer in North Dakota and winter in Mexico.

Birds begin return flight to their winter homes.

Fifty to sixty days after hatching, the young fly off to other areas.

JANUARY · FEBRUARY · MARCH · DECEMBER · NOVEMBER · OCTOBER · SEPTEMBER · AUGUST · JULY

While birds come in an astonishing variety of sizes, shapes, and colors, they all share a common need to feed and breed. These twin forces give rise to a life with a yearly cycle of courtship, mating, nesting, and raising of young.

Take the mallard, for example. In many ways, its life is typical of North American migratory birds. Mallards winter in a wide zone that stretches north from Mexico to southern Ohio. Those that live in the southernmost part of the range begin their migration north in February. By this point, the birds have formed breeding pairs after elaborate courtship rituals that include gestures such as bill- and tail-shaking *(pages 48-49)*.

Flying in flocks ranging from ten to two hundred birds, the mallards head north, following well-traveled

> *"My question, answer in the fewest words, What sort of life is it among the birds?"*
>
> — ARISTOPHANES

First of paired birds arrive in breeding area late in month.

Females choose nesting sites and begin laying their eggs.

APRIL

Eggs hatch after incubation period of twenty-five to twenty-nine days.

MAY

JUNE

First of breeding birds begin to molt; replacement of basic head-body feathers takes three weeks.

For mallards, egg-laying marks the end of pair bonds. The drakes part with their mates, congregating with other males to feed. The females incubate their eggs, taking an hour or two off in the afternoon to feed.

The ducklings hatch a month later, each weighing about an ounce. Within twelve hours, these precocial birds *(page 58)* can fend for themselves, trekking up to one and a half miles to reach water. After forty-two days, hatchlings begin to fly.

In summer—often in July—the adults start to molt, replacing their old, worn feathers with new sets. For the next month, both males and females remain flightless—this is typical of waterfowl species—seeking sanctuary in large flocks in marshes and other trackless areas. But with the arrival of autumn and the return of cooler temperatures, it is time once again to migrate.

Fighting storms, disorientation, and the rigors of long hours of flight, the birds navigate their way back south. Some die along the way from exhaustion; others may succumb to predators, hunters, or disease. But the birds that do succeed in returning to their wintering grounds in Mexico will spend the next few months fattening up, choosing a mate, and preparing for the journey north again the following spring.

A few of these mallards will live for more than five years—at least one is known to have survived into its twenties—but, in the hard avian world, most of them are lucky to complete this yearly cycle more than twice in a lifetime.

flight paths. Along the way, they feed on cultivated grain, aquatic plants, frogs, and small fish. The first of the migrating mallards pass the Canadian border in late March. Some will continue as far as Alaska, their arrival timed to coincide with spring thaw.

Shortly after arriving at their summer homes, the mallards choose nesting sites with heavy grass cover, usually in marshes and flooded fields or near shallow ponds. The females lay an average clutch of eight eggs in nests of cattails, reeds, and grasses.

Courtship Rites

Spring skies fill with bird song and puzzling aerial displays. This is the mating season, and birds are at their most visible and vocal. It's a time for males to "strut their stuff," showing off their genetic splendor to attract the attention of females. It's not an easy time—males exhaust themselves, lose weight, and run the risk of attracting predators as well as mates by flashing their plumage. But to further the species, this burst of exaggerated behavior is necessary.

Courtship displays are as varied as birds themselves. Some are simple, if not outright blunt. Male song sparrows announce themselves by colliding with females in midair. Songbirds such as mockingbirds and brown thrashers rely on elaborate melodies, and noises needn't be harmonious to be effective: The turkey gets results by rattling its quills, the pigeon by slapping its wings together over its back, and the common nighthawk by making buzzing sounds with its flight feathers.

Most males display special plumage, which may include gaudy plumes, crests, and pennants. Some birds, such as the sage grouse and greater prairie chicken, go all out, staging fancy dances in specific areas, or leks. Their ritual involves

Showmanship Rituals
Courtship displays include (1) the touching of bills, or "billing," of wandering albatrosses; (2) the exotic dancing of whooping cranes; (3) the colorful air sac of a greater prairie chicken; (4) the inflatable red throat pouch of a magnificent frigatebird; and (5) the joint water dance of western grebes.
Left: A great egret's breeding plumage announces the bird's availability to a mate.

males inflating air sacs on their necks and creating popping and booming sounds. Females approach the lek and choose mates from among the aspiring participants that have gathered in an area up to two hundred yards wide and a half mile long. Invariably, the male at the most central position in the lek proves to be the most attractive to females and sires the most young.

THE REASONS FOR RITUALS

What's behind these rituals? It's all about choosing the best possible mate. For closely related species, distinctive rituals such as unique songs can help prevent confusion that might otherwise lead to cross-bred sterile hybrids. Males and females of the same species often resemble one another as well. The male and female northern flicker, for example, look identical except for black "mustache" marks. In one study, a researcher painted the marks on a female, which was mistaken as an intruder by its mate and promptly attacked.

Where the sexes are clearly differentiated (sexual dimorphism), males are flamboyantly arrayed during the mating season. The Anna's hummingbird, for example, goes to unusual lengths to show off its flashy purple coloration, angling itself into the sunlight to provide the desired female with the best possible effect.

Apart from behavior, there are hard and fast physiological grounds for courtship displays. They stimulate ovulation in the female and reinforce the male's interest in mating through a form of self-stimulation.

The Polygamous Bird

The vast majority of birds are monogamous. But monogamy, which comes in different forms, is not for everyone. With polygyny, a single male mates with multiple females, each of which mates only with him. The breeding male, such as the redwing blackbird below, benefits by passing on genes to many females; the females benefit by mating with the male with the best genes. Polyandry, in which one female mates with several males, is rarer than polygyny and often involves a reversal of sexual roles. Ornithologists are now using DNA testing to determine whether youngsters in a given nest are indeed

the progeny of the adult birds attending to them. What they have discovered so far is that with birds such as indigo buntings and tree swallows, up to half of the offspring are sired by males other than the ones that take on responsibility for their raising.

This is important because males and females need to synchronize their physical readiness to mate for fertilization to occur. Gonads and other reproductive organs become enlarged during mating. The testes of a duck, for example, may swell to one tenth of the bird's overall weight. Mutual readiness helps reduce the time the birds carry this added bulk. Even for birds, timing is everything.

The Architecture of Nests

The quintessential cup-shaped nest perched on a branch is actually the exception in the bird world. Nests come in every imaginable size and shape, from the simple bowl built by a mockingbird in less than a day to the huge platform constructed by a bald eagle in a treetop, which is added to year after year until it collapses under its own weight. Most nests, however, have the same purpose: keeping eggs and nestlings safe from predators and the elements.

STAYING SAFE

The simplest way to frustrate predators is to put the nest out of reach. The hermit hummingbird, for example, suspends its nest from a cord of matted spiderwebs attached to a leaf or branch, carefully weighting it so it doesn't tip. In a similar approach, the tailorbird of southeast Asia chooses a leaf at the end of a slender branch and laces together the edges with plant fibers or animal hair to form a funnel. Some waterbirds, such as grebes, build anchored floating nests of twigs and branches that bob gently out-of-reach offshore, while belted kingfishers dig tunnels up to five feet long in muddy banks, stashing their eggs in chambers at the ends.

If the nest can't be kept out of reach, birds try to design it so it won't be spotted in the first place. Least terns set their eggs in shallow depressions in the sand and camouflage them with pebbles and bits of grass; kinglets carefully cover their nests with lichens so they resemble the stubs of branches. For some birds, building no nest at all is a way to avoid drawing attention to the eggs. A plover lays its eggs directly on bare ground and the white tern is famous for neatly balancing a single egg in the fork of a tree branch.

Perhaps the most original way to keep a nest safe is to count on others to protect it. Sparrows will sometimes attach their nests to the sides of eagle nests. The eagles may tolerate the smaller birds because they act as resident burglar alarms, letting out distress calls if intruders approach; the larger birds then fend off the predator. Other birds make their homes among stinging insects—one

Home Security
Inventive nest building helps birds keep predators at bay.

BALTIMORE ORIOLE
A woven nest dangling from a tree branch

WESTERN GREBE
A nest that is a floating raft of branches and twigs

type of tropical woodpecker will actually build its nest inside a spherical nest belonging to ants.

KEEPING WARM

Many large birds do little to protect their eggs from the elements, counting on their own body heat to keep the eggs warm. Small perching birds, however, often go to great pains to shelter their eggs. Many tropical birds build covered nests to keep out the rain. The weaverbird of Africa, perhaps the king of nest builders, constructs a tightly woven, comma-shaped nest with an entrance at the bottom. The ruby-throated hummingbird covers its nesting area with saliva to help solidify the structure.

The snug home of a small songbird may require several materials

Anything Goes
Most birds have favorite nesting materials—from mud to their own saliva. But some will use literally anything they can get their beaks on. One red-tailed hawk's nest was found with nails, glass, adhesive tape, and several pieces of old inner tubes mixed among its twigs.

in its construction. The American robin, for example, builds a structure of twigs, then plasters the inside with mud and lines it with a warm layer of leaves and grasses. Feathers make another cozy lining. All the eider duck needs to do to feather its nest is pull out beakfuls of its own down.

Nests can sometimes be overbuilt. The American goldfinch nest, constructed of grasses and moss and lined with thistle down, is so watertight that it can collect rainwater and drown the fledglings.

NEST-BUILDING HEADACHES

Many birds invest enormous energy in preparing a nest. The constructions of a mud nest involves transporting the material a beakful at a time, carefully shaping and compacting it. Woven nests often require delicately splitting plant fibers, soaking them in water, and knotting them together. Excavated nests involve endless scrabbling with beaks and feet. Of course there's a shortcut: Some birds dispense with all the work and simply take over nests that have been built by others.

KILLDEER
A nest that is nothing but a hollow and some pebbles

MARSH WREN
A football-shaped nest suspended in a bed of reeds

51

Deadly Nest Behavior

Some birds disguise their eggs to look like those of the host. The top egg in this red warbler's nest is actually one laid by a European cuckoo—and can vary from bright blue to darkly speckled in accordance with the appearance of the host's eggs.

Building a nest and raising birds from hatched eggs to fledglings takes a lot of energy. But, as some birds demonstrate, there is a simple way to avoid all the bother: Leave the job for another bird to do.

Known as brood parasitism, the practice of laying eggs in the nests of other species and leaving the rearing of young to foster parents offers obvious advantages: It maximizes the ability of a bird to reproduce successfully as often as possible. Since the perpetrator is free of responsibility to rear chicks, the bird has the energy to create more eggs. Some parasitic species lay an average of one egg more than nonparasitic birds.

Not all birds are duped by an extra egg in the nest. Some, such as warblers, vireos, and song sparrows, don't seem to mind accommodating uninvited guests, but others—robins and blue jays, for instance—instinctively eject strange eggs from the nest. In a few cases, the birds may even build a new nest on top of the old one. Still other foster parents will refuse to feed parasite chicks, which then starve to death.

Ornithologists are unsure how the practice originated. Some believe that it began in the tropics where predators frequently raid nests, causing birds to seek a new nest for another brood. By avoiding the proverbial "putting all your eggs in one basket," a bird also can help ensure that at least one of its young will survive long enough to leave the nest.

The eggs of a brown-headed cowbird tend to hatch a day or two earlier than those of its typical host, giving the newborns a decided advantage in claiming food from the foster parent. Here, a cowbird chick competes with an outmatched baby yellow warbler.

Something is obviously amiss in this nest of reed warblers. A cuckoo chick, a notorious brood parasite, dwarfs the diminutive cup-shaped shelter.

bird's chicks. Baby honeyguides have special fanglike hooks at the end of their bills. When the birds hatch, they instinctively begin biting and frequently kill the rightful occupants of the nest. As the birds mature, the hooks drop off. Other invaders push the host bird's eggs out of the nest—an instinct that disappears within a few days of a foster bird hatching.

Brood parasitism is far from widespread. Less than 1 percent of all bird species engage in the activity. In North America, the best known example is the brown-headed cowbird, which lays eggs in the nests of more than two hundred species of birds. But the award for the most skilled practitioner of brood parasitism worldwide must go to the cuckoo, which carefully scouts out nests for its nefarious activities, often choosing ones that are an egg short of a complete clutch. Some cuckoos can even lay eggs that are colored to match the host's own. These mimetic eggs make the detection of the intruder eggs virtually impossible.

Raising an interloper's egg takes its toll. In the best of situations, the host parents merely expend extra energy feeding another chick. In many cases, though, a host bird's own chicks die as the greedy parasite reduces their food intake—leaving desperate foster parents to feed intruding chicks that rapidly grow to sizes much larger than themselves.

The instinct for survival stirs strongly among brood parasites and tends, in some cases, to the deadly. To increase their chances of living, newly hatched honeyguides and cuckoos kill the host

Eggs and Incubation

Fluffing its feathers and huddling down over its single egg, an albatross settles in to wait—for eighty days without a break. A tortoise, on the other hand, lays a hundred eggs and promptly abandons them. Both the albatross and the tortoise have evolved ways to maximize the number of offspring they raise. Reptiles lay large numbers of eggs, of which only a few will survive, while birds lay only a few eggs to start with and invest enormous amounts of energy in protecting them until they hatch.

EGGS BIG AND SMALL

Set next to an ostrich egg, the diminutive hummingbird egg looks like a marble beside a melon. In general, the size of a bird egg corresponds to the size of the bird itself. However, some birds lay surprisingly large eggs for their size. The kiwi of New Zealand lays an egg a full quarter of its body weight. And not all eggs are "egg-shaped." Some, such as those of owls, are almost spherical. Others, the eggs of common murres, for example, are pointed at one end, preventing them from rolling off the cliff ledges where they are laid.

The wide array of colors and patterns of many bird eggs sometimes serves for camouflage purposes. A robin's blue egg blends into the background in the dappled shade of the forest, while the speckled egg of the ringed plover matches the pebbles among which it is laid. White eggs, the most vulnerable to predators, are generally laid only by birds that hide their eggs deep inside a cavity or keep their eggs continuously covered during the entire incubation period.

THE MAKING OF AN EGG

The creation of an egg inside the bird's body is a several-step process. When first released from the ovary of a female bird, the egg consists of only the yolk and the fertilized germinal cell. As it travels through the chambers of the oviduct, layers of albumen (white) are added assembly-line fashion. Finally, in the uterine section of the oviduct, the hard shell is formed and the pigment is added. (Dotted patterns are formed if the egg sits still in the oviduct as the pigment is applied, streaks and splotches if it keeps moving.) Many birds lay eggs in the early morning, possibly because the period of inactivity during the night is best for the formation of the shell.

Personalized Eggs

Common murres live in colonies of thousands, yet each bird is able to identify its own eggs. That's because every bird's egg has a distinct color and pattern of dots and splotches. In experiments, the murres reject any eggs that don't have their own individual pattern.

The number of eggs in a clutch can vary from the single egg of an albatross to the set of up to eighteen laid by a partridge. Although the size of a clutch is fairly consistent within a species, it can vary somewhat based on a number of complex factors—including the availability of food in a particular season and the age of the bird. In general, birds lay the number of eggs that they have the energy to incubate and the resources to feed.

All birds lay one egg at a time, often at intervals of twenty-four or forty-eight hours. Some simply stop laying at the requisite number, even if the eggs are pilfered. Other species keep right on laying if their eggs are removed—a trait that makes domestic chickens so useful.

INCUBATION
Most birds wait until all the eggs in the clutch have been laid before beginning the hard work of incuba-

Anatomy of an Egg
The yolk in the center of the egg, initially composed of white and yellow layers, provides nutrients to the developing chick. The yolk is surrounded by a protective layer of albumen and two shell membranes. Cords called chalaza anchor the inner layer of white, allowing the yolk to rotate inside it so the germinal, or fertilized, spot is always at the top. The porous calcium shell allows for the exchange of oxygen and waste gases. The air space at one end actually expands as moisture is lost through the shell, keeping the humidity at the right level. It's a delicate balance. If the air cell is too small, the chick will drown; if it is too big, the chick will be crowded and won't have enough room to maneuver when hatching.

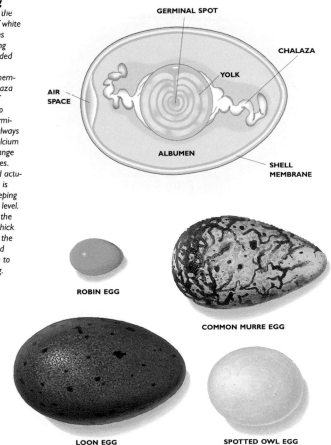

GERMINAL SPOT

CHALAZA

YOLK

AIR SPACE

ALBUMEN

SHELL MEMBRANE

ROBIN EGG

COMMON MURRE EGG

NORTHERN JACANA EGG

LOON EGG

SPOTTED OWL EGG

The blue-footed booby crouches atop its eggs, warming them with its feet.

For birds living in hot climates, incubating means keeping the eggs cool instead of warm. The common nighthawk will spend long hours crouched over the eggs, shading them with its wings, and some birds, such as killdeers, will wet their breast feathers and allow the water to drip onto the eggs.

Incubating is an exhausting job, and each species has its own scheme for how to share the work between the male and the female. While in many species the female has sole responsibility for incubating and must take breaks to feed, in some the female is faithfully fed by its mate. In a few species, such as the ostrich, it is the male that has sole charge. However, the most common pattern is for the male and female birds each to take shifts. Double-crested cormorants relieve each other every hour or two, while starlings alternate during the day, but at night the female alone takes care of incubation.

In the rare cases of polyandry—one female mates with more than one male—the male may be the

tion. For the eggs to develop properly, they must be kept warm no matter how chilled the surrounding air. Many species have special brood patches on their bellies to help transfer their body heat to the eggs. The birds lose feathers from these areas during the breeding season or deliberately pluck them out and the skin becomes suffused with extra blood vessels.

Incubating is more than just sitting. Periodically the bird must rise and shift the eggs in the nest so they are warmed and aerated evenly. Moving the eggs also ensures that each embryo is rotated; otherwise, it can stick to the membranes inside the shell and fail to hatch.

The Chemical Threat

In her 1962 book *Silent Spring*, biologist Rachel Carson warned of the threat of a continent without songbirds. The culprit was broadcast spraying of chemicals to battle Dutch elm disease and crop parasites. Pesticides and herbicides can kill small birds directly and have insidious toxic effects on birds higher up in the food chain. Accumulated in the birds' bodies, pesticides and herbicides affect their calcium metabolism, causing abnormally thin only incubator. In other cases, such as the spotted sandpiper, the female incubates one of her clutches and leaves the incubation of her other eggs to her mates.

Sitting on the eggs is the most common incubating method, but some birds have developed original alternatives. The male emperor penguin sets a single egg on top of its feet and covers the egg with a flap of skin, keeping it toasty warm for eight to nine weeks—despite temperatures that may drop as low as minus 70°F.

FROM EMBRYO TO CHICK

Inside the warm, protective environment of the egg, the germinal spot gradually develops into a chick. First a tiny beating heart appears, then a head, and finally the body and limbs. As the chick develops, it gradually consumes the yolk and white of the egg, and its waste is collected in a special sac. The porous shell allows the chick to breathe by exchanging water vapor and carbon dioxide from the inside for oxygen from the outside.

eggshells that may shatter as the eggs are laid. Such weakened shells almost drove peregrine falcons into extinction. Pressure from the environmental movement led to a ban on the use of organochlorines in North America in 1972. However, they are still widely used in other parts of the world. More recent chemical substitutes such as organophosphates don't accumulate in the same way, but can be extremely toxic to birds that ingest them.

A Natural Warming Oven
The malleefowl of Australia works hard to keep its eggs warm, but not in the usual way. The birds lay their eggs in huge mounds of plant materials, allowing the heat generated by the decomposing vegetation to warm them. The adult birds regularly check the temperature, opening or closing the mounds as necessary.

A day or two before the chick is ready to hatch, it sticks its beak into the air gap at the end of the egg and starts to breathe normally, letting out feeble peeps. Then, it hammers a tiny hole in the shell, rests, and adds a ring of holes around the end of the egg. Finally, the chick pops the end off the egg and struggles into the world.

Hatching is a surprisingly tough job that can take up to three days. The chicks of some species, such as the roseate spoonbill, have a special egg tooth to help them break through shell. This feature is lost shortly after hatching. Many birds also have special hatching muscles in their necks that atrophy once the chicks have pecked themselves free.

One puzzle of the bird world is why the parent birds, having so carefully tended the eggs as they developed, don't also assist the struggling chicks to break out of their prisons. Perhaps, as some ornithologists suggest, hatching is a chick's first important survival test.

Raising Their Young

When a parent brings food, a chick cranes its neck, bill pointed upward. If the chick's eyes are closed, the chick will gape when it senses the vibrations of the parent returning to the nest. The bright-colored interior of the chick's mouth signals the parent where to insert the food. Once the chick reaches fledgling age, the bright lining fades.

During the incubation period, the parent birds' primary responsibility is to keep the eggs warm and protected. Once the chicks hatch, they must be fed and kept warm. In addition, the nest must be kept clean to prevent disease and ward off parasites.

Young birds fall into two main categories, called precocial and altricial. Precocial chicks are capable of fending for themselves as soon as, or very shortly after, they are hatched, depending on the species. Altricial chicks are born naked, blind, and too weak to stand up. All perching birds are altricial; birds such as ducks, sandpipers, and cranes tend to be precocial.

While birds are warm-blooded as adults, chicks are born cold-blooded, leaving them vulnerable to fluctuating temperatures. Brooding behavior varies according to both temperature and precipitation. During the formative period and until the chicks can regulate their own body temperature, the parents need to brood, protecting their young with their own body heat in extreme cold or preventing them from overheating in very hot conditions.

Parents instinctively know how long to brood—usually most of the day and all

Although precocial birds, such as the mute swan cygnets at left, can fend for themselves shortly after birth, they usually remain in visual or vocal contact with the mother. Altricial birds, such as painted buntings (inset), may take weeks before they can fend for themselves.

night initially, then decreasingly during the day.

Feeding keeps the parents very busy. In some instances, males that took no part in the nest-building or incubation assume the main responsibility for finding food. Most chicks are fed insects or small creatures such as spiders, snails, and worms with high concentrations of calcium, protein, and other growth-promoting nutrients. Because this type of food also contains fluid, young birds do not need to drink. Collecting food is hard work. House wrens make as many as five hundred trips a day to the nest with food.

DEFENDING THEIR YOUNG

Most parents vigorously protect their young if there is a reasonable chance of defense. Otherwise, they abandon the nest. To make life harder for predators, some species build nests near beehives, others close to tree ants; in some instances, birds seek trees near human habitation for nesting. In the face of a serious threat to the nestlings, some birds, such as the red-tailed hawk, scoop up their young with their claws or toes and head for safer ground. Chicks that sense impending danger will crouch in the nest to make themselves invisible if they are unable to flee.

A clean nest not only helps to guard

Deception is the better part of valor: A killdeer feigns a broken wing to lure a predator away from its nest.

against disease and parasites, it also blends into its surroundings and is less conspicuous to predators. Adult birds usually dispose of eggshells shortly after hatching so that their chicks will not injure themselves on the sharp edges.

Most bird species are diligent about excrement disposal. The waste of many nestlings is discharged in a fecal sac made of tough mucous membrane. Once defecation has occurred, the parent will pick up the sac and drop it away from the nest. Swallows let go of the sacs over water, wrens place them on tree branches away from nests, while prairie warblers actually eat the sacs, using the remains as a source of badly needed nourishment. Birds often become malnourished during the rearing period.

The length of the nesting period of altricial species varies, depending on factors such as the duration of incubation and the size of the species. Along with the instinctive maturation behavior that prompts a chick to leave the nest, factors such as weather, hunger, accidents, and parental nudging all have an impact. Some parent birds entice their young to leave by holding food far enough away from them that they are obliged to exit the nest in order to reach it.

A Place of Their Own

To humans, bird song seems the essence of peace and harmony. In fact, it may be a clarion call to battle. Singing is just one of the means employed by birds to conquer or defend territory. And territory is central to avian society.

Territory confers multiple and decisive benefits. A good territory is full of food and well protected. The owner thus enjoys superior chances of attracting a mate and breeding. The brood will be well fed and will most likely survive to independence. In this way, the genes of the fittest will be passed on to benefit the species. Some species, such as robins, are so strongly territorial that only males with a home range are physically able to copulate.

Except in a few species such as phalaropes and jacanas, establishing a territory is usually a male pursuit—and it isn't easy. In fact, many males never achieve a range of their own and are consequently doomed to bachelorhood. Those that do find a place to settle are successful because they arrive early from migration, benefit from the death of previous occupants, or push less assertive males out of their way.

Bird Territoriality
A bird's territory may vary from a few square feet to many square miles, but birds have definite ideas about where it starts and ends. A robin, for example, typically has a territory of roughly a quarter of an acre, which he will defend against competing males.

TERRITORY SIZE AND SPACING

The size of a bird's territory depends on various factors. In addition to the age, sex, size, and even individual assertiveness of the bird, there is the pressing issue of food availability. Prey density decrees that larger birds need more space than smaller ones, carnivores more than insectivores.

Ranges may be flexible. Birds shrink their territory to accommodate arrivals of the same species during times of plenty and hold fast or even expand the boundaries during times of want. Some birds use a given territory for a season, while others return to the same place year after year. There are even winter territories: Snowy owls guard hunting domains in the coldest months of the year and red-headed woodpeckers defend caches of food.

The type of territory also plays its part. Species such as the chimney swift defend only the immediate area around the nest. Herbivores are tied to specific feeding areas: the mockingbird defends the bush containing its favorite berries. Larger carnivores, such as golden eagles, need to patrol vast hunting ranges as large as thirty-five square miles. Other sample ranges for birds are shown in the chart at right below.

Spacing of territories is important for all birds. While a given tract of forest may contain a dense concentration of diverse species, birds of the same feather generally keep a distance from one another. This assures more peaceful breeding conditions. It also helps to protect the species from predators. When crows, cats, or raccoons raid a nest, they look for more of the same in the immediate vicinity.

What appears to be open air space is in fact an unseen quilt of territorial divisions as complex as a map of medieval Europe. Even among the same species, the size of territories varies; the most fit birds carve out large areas and the weaker ones are relegated to the fringes. Some birds, such as the phainopepla of the southwest United States, maintain separate breeding and feeding territories.

MAINTAINING TERRITORIES

It's one thing to define a territory; it's another to maintain it. Birds keep trespassers at bay by various methods, principally by voice. A seaside sparrow was observed singing 395 songs in one hour to scare off unwanted males. And in one experiment, male red-winged blackbirds that were made mute experienced greater trespassing on their turfs. Once their voices were restored, they quickly reestablished their territories.

Birds also strike threatening postures to protect their territories. When an interloper invades the territory of a male yellow wagtail, for example, it puffs up its breast feathers and sways from side to side. Male herring gulls rip out beakfuls of grass from the ground and engage in tugging matches with their adversaries.

A few species of birds even resort to using physical force. Penguins have been observed hitting intruders with their flippers and pecking until blood is drawn. And a four-foot-tall sandhill crane was once observed driving a caribou out of its territory.

TYPICAL TERRITORY SIZES	
STARLING	0.0002 acre
LEAST FLYCATCHER	0.07 acre
RED-WINGED BLACKBIRD	0.8 acre
OVENBIRD	2.5 acres
WESTERN MEADOWLARK	22 acres
RED-TAILED HAWK	256 acres
BALD EAGLE	640 acres

Note: The ranges of bird species can vary depending on habitat.

The Communal Bird

Most birds are loners at heart, but certain species find their strength in numbers. About 13 percent of bird species make their homes in large communities that share a nesting area. Many of these species are marine birds such as gannets, thousands of which may stake out a rocky island and squeeze in their nests side by side. Birds that live in colonies tend to be those with food sources that are constantly on the move—schools of fish in the case of gannets, swarms of insects for cliff swallows, another colonial nester. For these birds, there is little point in defending individual hunting territories when the prey itself doesn't stay put.

Communal life has its drawbacks, such as transmission of disease and parasites along with fights over food and mates. In trying to explain why some birds live this way, researchers have looked for benefits that might outweigh these costs. One possible advantage is increased safety from predators. In a large community, each bird can afford to be less vigilant with so many others also watching and one bird's alarm call can send the whole flock reeling into the sky in a show of intimidation. And even if a predator does manage to rob a nest, each bird faces only a small chance of its nest being the one that is singled out from the surrounding thousands of others.

Cliff swallows build colonies of mud nests, cementing them to the face of rocks.

Many birds that nest in colonies also forage together, and the colonies can serve as information centers for sharing news about the changing locations of food supplies. For example, when a cliff swallow returns to its nesting site with food, other birds will accompany it back out, following its lead to discover the source of the nourishment.

Recent research on why some birds live in colonies suggests that there may be more to explaining the phenomenon than simply a question of costs versus benefits. One researcher at York University in Toronto, Ontario, has proposed that colonial life increases birds' sexual success rates. Although most colony-dwelling birds are monogamous, they do copulate with birds other than their primary mates. Such extra-pair copulations appear to benefit both the males and the females *(page 49)*. Nesting in groups may simply increase those opportunities.

Another process that may lead indirectly to communal life is the evaluation of nesting sites. A study of kittiwakes that nest on cliffs along the coast of Brittany showed that each bird will return to the same nesting site year after year if it finds the location to be a good one. Those dissatisfied with their site will go looking for another, actually inspecting the nests of other birds to check the health of their young. Where other birds are found to be doing well, they will join the community, swelling its ranks.

King penguins in Antarctica congregate in colonies of tens of thousands, stretching as far as the eye can see. When they huddle, the temperature at the middle of a group can rise by as much as 20°F.

The Migratory Quest

From Egyptian hieroglyphs to biblical verse, some of the world's earliest texts depict the mysterious comings and goings of birds. Today scientific knowledge has greatly expanded on those early observations; yet, while migrations have been minutely clocked and plotted, an aura of mystery about them remains.

Migration is a spectacular event that arises from the very unspectacular need of an animal to feed itself. The origins of bird migration lie beyond our grasp. Perhaps the shifting climatic changes brought about by glaciation forced birds from the north into equatorial regions for part of the year. And no doubt at some point in avian evolution, risk-taking individuals from the tropics ventured northward during summer months to take advantage of a bonanza of food, long daylight hunting hours, and increased breeding space. Such

opportunism involved trade-offs: the exhausting round-trip journey versus the probability of surviving. Yet the gamble paid off for many, and still does. Although most tropical birds stay at home, each year some 150 species shuttle between Central and North America, even though half their numbers may perish along the way.

In North America and Europe, birds use well established flyways, some of which may have emerged in the waning days of the last Ice Age. There are four in North America: the Pacific, Central, Mississippi, and Atlantic. All are food-rich paths to warmer climes. In Europe, Gibraltar is the embarkation port for Africa.

Generally, large soaring species stay over land, riding rising thermals. Flapping migratory species fly directly across open water to Yucatan. Several species of plovers

Theories vary on why birds such as these snow geese fly in V-formation. Perhaps the practice is a way to gain extra lift from the wingtip vortices produced by nearby birds or a means to avoid in-flight collisions.

PACIFIC
MISSISSIPPI
CENTRAL
ATLANTIC

and god-wits fly nonstop from Cape Cod to Trinidad, some twenty-five hundred miles.

Migrations may be as short as a blue grouse's descent from hilltop to valley floor at the onset of autumn or as epic as the Arctic tern's four-month odyssey from pole to pole. But all migrants share basic abilities: They know when to depart and where they're going.

Seasonal change has physical effects on birds. Alterations in temperature and light stimulate the pituitary and adrenal glands into releasing prolactin and corticosterone, two hormones that encourage fat storage. This is important: A small bird may lose nearly half its weight during the trip. Before the spring migration, hormones begin to enlarge the reproductive organs, which must be ready for action on arrival at the breeding grounds. Extreme restlessness and a reorientation of perching toward the direction of migration precede departure.

Flying as fast as they can, birds cover tremendous distances. Peregrine falcons have been known to fly eighteen hundred miles in twenty-four hours—averaging seventy-five miles per hour. The feats of hummingbirds are no less impressive.

Travel Routes
Birds in North America tend to migrate along a north–south axis following one of four flyways: Pacific, Mississippi, Central, or Atlantic.

The ruby-throated hummingbird, which weighs only a tenth of an ounce, leaves its home in eastern North America every fall and embarks on a two-thousand-mile trip to Central America. The epic voyage includes a six-hundred-mile nonstop crossing of the Gulf of Mexico. Many species fly in formation, such as a V, which may reduce wing vortex drag or aid communication. Young birds can benefit from the experience of older flyers, but in one case, the New Zealand bronzed cuckoo, novices rendezvous with their parents twenty-two hundred miles from home—without having followed the older birds.

Despite repeated experiments, scientists remain puzzled by the reason birds initially select particular breeding and feeding grounds. Once established, they become fixed destinations. After flying sometimes thousands of miles, most birds return to within a stone's throw of a previous nest, some to precisely the same tree. How do they find their way back?

NAVIGATION TOOLS

Birds use every trick in the navigational book. Sensitivity to light—through the eyes and even the skull—not only works as a calendar, but also as a clock. Birds always know what time it is and since each hour represents a 15° change in longitude, they always know where they are. Using shadows to determine the sun's height and direction, birds calculate its arc relative to the horizon; this angle gives them a reliable north–south axis—an inner solar compass. Most small birds migrate by night, avoiding predators, and spend daylight hours "refueling." Many large birds fly nonstop day and night. Nocturnal navigation is aided by the stars: Hatchlings are imprinted with a celestial map revolving around the north stars. Magnetic sensitivity—possibly due to small deposits of magnetite in the skull—also assist orientation. The earth's magnetic

One of the tools that ornithologists use to test the effects of stellar clues on a bird's ability to navigate is a funnel-shaped cone with an ink pad at the base. When the bird flutters against the side of the cone in response to artificially altered visual clues, it leaves telltale marks that can later be analyzed.

Scientists who studied migration once believed that birds used the moon as a navigational aid, but it now appears that stars provide the only celestial clues. Other factors, such as the earth's magnetic field, the angle of the sun, and even visual clues play a role in bird navigation.

calls, used as sonar, may be picked up in echoes off mountain walls. Some scientists, basing theories on behavior correlated to lunar cycles, even speculate that birds can sense minute variations in gravity. Given the earth's irregular shape, this may be an important indicator of place.

When approaching a destination, birds rely on visual cues to home in, although some, such as the leach's storm petrel, rely on their sense of smell to find their sites. Some seabirds would rather get a taste of home—sips of seawater tell them whether they're on the right track.

field varies in a regular angular pattern according to latitude. Using their sense of the horizontal and calculating the angle of the magnetic field against it, migrating birds always fly toward the acute angle, along a north–south magnetic axis.

Other talents narrow the margin of error still further. A sensitivity to changes in barometric pressure enables birds to evade poor weather and exploit tail winds created by warm or cold fronts. The ability to pick up ultralow-frequency sound waves may help birds on the wing detect such things as ocean waves breaking on a rocky shore, even at high altitudes. Their own

The King of the Migrators

The Arctic tern has made migration a way of life, flying from pole to pole for more than two hundred days of the year. The tern's journey takes it some eleven thousand miles from breeding areas in Greenland and northern Canada to feeding areas in South America and the Antarctic. The bird is in no hurry, often taking a figure-eight path across the Atlantic Ocean and stopping frequently to feed and rest along the way. During their circuitous trips, the terns probably experience more daylight than any other bird—spending parts of their year in the Arctic and the Antarctic at the time when each region is awash in continuous light.

Space–Age Tracking

In the mid-1990s, North American ornithologists were perplexed by the sudden decrease in the number of nesting Swainson's hawks in many of its North American habitats. After eliminating the possibility of local factors contributing to the mysterious decline of the previously common bird, experts concluded that problems must exist somewhere along its migration routes or in its wintering areas. The challenge: How to trace the flight patterns of a bird with a travel route that stretches from Alaska all the way to the Pampas of Argentina?

In the past, keeping track of birds usually involved placing an identifying band on a bird's leg and then hoping it might be found dead somewhere along its migration route—a century-old technique for which success depended to a large degree on chance. With those hit-and-miss efforts, the number of Swainson's hawks could well have withered until the birds faced extinction before the reasons for their disappearance were uncovered.

However, since the mid-1980s, ornithologists have had a new tool at their disposal: satellite telemetry. This space-age tracking system utilizes satellite technology to monitor the migratory habits of birds that have been equipped with lightweight platform transmitter terminals (PTTs). Weighing no more than 3 to 5 percent of the bird's total body weight, these tiny transmitters have been designed so as not to impede the bird's mobility. The transmitter sends a signal to a satellite, which relays information on the bird's location to a ground station.

Using this high-tech tracking system, the ornithologists concerned about the plight of Swainson's hawks followed the raptors' migration across nine states and provinces, through Central America, and right down to Argentina. When researchers made a trip to the hawks' Argentinean roosting sites in 1996, the scientists were shocked to find the carcasses of some four thousand birds. The reason: Grasshoppers that the birds ate had feasted on crops sprayed with toxic chemicals to cut down on ravaging insects. Once introduced into the food chain, the poison devastated the hawk population. The ensuing conservation efforts by Argentina, Canada, the United States, and the agrochemical industry, which involved educating farmers

in alternative methods of crop management, helped keep the Swainson's hawk off the endangered species list.

But keeping birds safe from humans isn't the only application of this type of tracking. Sometimes the reverse is needed. In 1995, for example, twenty-four people were killed when a radar surveillance jet crashed after impact with large birds in flight over Alaska. The U.S. Department of Defense is now using satellite-based tracking to study bird movements near some of its military bases.

A case in point is the Naval Air Station Fallon in the Lahontan Valley near Reno, Nevada. Here, the navy's top guns have to share air space along the Pacific flyway with some 400,000 birds, including pelicans, swans, geese, and ducks. While a small bird might cause minimal damage to a jet, hitting a fifteen-pound pelican at 550 miles per hour can destroy the plane in a blink of an eye. By fitting a number of pelicans with transmitters, wildlife biologists and navy air-traffic controllers hope to be able to predict the flight patterns of the birds well enough to steer pilots away from potentially hazardous encounters with the birds.

As with all technology, satellite-based tracking is becoming more and more refined. Lighter platform transmitter terminals mean that smaller species of birds can be monitored. With the development of Global Positioning System (GPS) technology, researchers have even greater accuracy; the GPS network of twenty-four satellites can pinpoint a location on the ground or in the air within a hundred yards. Meteorological and acoustic sensors will soon be able to record crucial data ranging from climate conditions to species interrelationships. In this brave new world of ornithology, Big Brother is a friend who is always watching.

Surveillance by Satellite
With satellite tracking, a bird such as the peregrine falcon (opposite) carries a lightweight Argos transmitter strapped to its back. The transmitter emits a signal picked up by one of a series of satellites in a polar orbit that provides full global coverage (below). The data is stored until the satellite comes within range of a ground station on earth, at which point it transmits its information to the tracking center for relaying to biologists' personal computers.

Bird Talk

Like all animals, birds need to communicate, whether to their mates, their young, or their enemies. Where birds stand out is in the sheer beauty and variety of the sounds they produce. Ornithologists roughly categorize the vocal utterances of birds as either "calls" or "songs." Calls are a syllable or two in length, each with a single set form. Songs are much longer and more complex. While almost all birds make some kind of calls, it is primarily songbirds, a suborder of perching birds, that delight our ears in the woods in springtime.

Many birds, such as this marsh wren, have a favorite perch where they sing, typically at a safe distance from the nest. Songbirds may spend up to ten hours a day singing, but dawn is a favorite moment, perhaps because a song carries well in the cool morning air.

among different species, and the alarm call of one might send nearby birds of a number of species into the air. There are also species that use their calls as personal name tags. King penguins, which live in huge colonies, can recognize their young from among thousands of others by their individual calls.

Making and responding to calls seems to be instinctive—baby birds will crouch down in response to a parent's warning call when they are only hours old. However, there is also evidence that calls are not made by reflex every time a bird spots danger. Studies show that some birds won't make alarm calls at all in the absence of a companion bird to serve as an audience. Pine siskins in an open field where they can stay in sight of each other make fewer calls than those living in dense foliage where vision is impeded.

CALLS

A "brirb-brirb" call from a mother greater prairie chicken will bring its young chick scurrying toward it. But a shrill warning call made by the mother will freeze the same chick in its tracks. Bird calls are generally used for this kind of social purpose: to warn of danger or to allow members of a flock on the move to locate each other.

Bird calls are generally very much the same for all members of a species. They may even be similar

BIRD SONG

Bird song, generally done only by the male bird, has two main functions: to establish territory and attract a mate. A proficient and vigorous song can indicate to a rival that the bird is a force to be reckoned with. As a courtship ritual, a bird's song can simply advertise availability as a fit mate, but some ornithologists also believe that song actually stimulates the reproductive cycle of the female bird. Studies of budgerigars, for example, found that male song promotes ovarian development in the females. Once the spring breeding period is over and male birds have mated and established their territory, they generally sing less.

In contrast to calls, the learning of bird song is a more complex process. A male white-crowned sparrow spends its first few weeks

Song Duos

You wouldn't know that the "cheen-cherry-gwee" song of Central American wrens is produced by two separate birds unless you actually saw them. The first two parts are sung by one member of the pair and the other adds "gwee." The sequence is then repeated over and over in a seamless duet. Certain members of about a dozen bird families engage in this kind of duet singing.

listening to other male birds and then begins to twitter, much like a human baby starts babbling. Then, the sparrow begins to experiment with notes that resemble real song. At a little under a year, the singing crystallizes as a full adult song. Research has shown that this process involves elements of both instinct and learning.

Experiments with birds that have been isolated from birth show that

Nonvocal Communication

Calls and songs are the preferred means of communication for most birds, but some species communicate without using their voices at all. The ruffed grouse (*right*) generates a thunderous drumming sound with its wings that can be heard at a distance of a quarter mile. Common nighthawks make whirring noises as the air rushes through their feathers during courtship rituals. And storks, which are completely mute, communicate by clacking their upper and lower bills together.

without a chance to hear an adult model during a critical sensitive period early in life, birds will never learn to sing normally. Similarly, deaf birds that never hear themselves sing are denied the benefits of practice and do not develop normal song. The studies also show that the learned aspects of song contain essential elements that give a particular song its unique, identifiable qualities. Played back to birds in the wild, the abnormal songs are virtually ignored.

But bird song is never entirely learned. Birds seem to be born with some hard-wired template of their species' song. Isolated in a lab, birds learn the song of their own species rather than another one if exposed to recordings of both. If exposed only to the inappropriate foreign song, most birds will learn it imperfectly—unless they are of a species so expert in the art of mimicry that they can dupe even avian ears with their flawless imitations *(pages 74-75)*.

Bird songs are generally similar within a species and can be an invaluable clue in identifying a hidden bird. However, the fact that bird song is partially learned means that there is some flexibility within the basic model. Some species have actually developed local dialects. White-crowned sparrows that live in Berkeley, California, for example, start their song with one or two pure whistles, while those on a nearby San Francisco army base opt for a whistle followed by a buzz. Individual birds can even improvise to some extent by rearranging elements of the song. Although this rearrangement doesn't affect the basic message, it may serve to impress the listener. Recordings have been made of individual song sparrows singing up to twenty different songs.

THE VOCAL SYSTEM

Humans produce sounds with the help of vocal cords that lie inside the larynx. Birds, however, have a vocal organ, called the syrinx, located down in the chest cavity. The syrinx contains two highly elastic membranes stretched tight like drum skins. The vibrations of these tympaniform membranes can be precisely controlled by muscles in the wall of the syrinx. The membranes can even be made

A Bird's Sound Apparatus
A bird's vocal organ, called the syrinx, is a chamber located where the two bronchi enter the trachea, or windpipe. Tympaniform membranes vibrate within the chamber, controlled by muscles in the syrinx walls.

TRACHEA

TYMPANIFORM MEMBRANE

BRONCHI

to vibrate at different rates to produce two simultaneous and unrelated notes.

Song Analysis
Musical notes and word mnemonics, as shown at top for the white-throated sparrow, are still useful in learning bird songs. Modern spectrograms like the one shown at bottom chart time on one axis and frequency on the other, allowing more accurate scientific analysis of bird songs.

The overall pitch of a bird's voice is influenced by the length of the windpipe, in the same way that a flute has a deeper sound than a piccolo. Some birds with particularly deep voices even have lengths of windpipe coiled up inside their sternums. Other species have special air sacs that amplify sound. The sage grouse, for example, has an inflatable air sac in its neck that enables it to produce its booming call.

Despite these variations, the difference in songs among species is not primarily due to differences in the vocal apparatus. Songbirds do have more developed syringal muscles than other birds, but the secret of their success seems to lie in the complexity of the network of brain nuclei in the forebrain devoted to song production.

STUDYING BIRD SONG

The impressive variety of bird songs has long intrigued scientists and nature-lovers alike, and the tools for study at their disposal are constantly improving. The first recordings of bird song were made in Germany in 1889. Since then, the development of portable tape recorders along with parabolic and directional microphones *(page 85)* has allowed scientists to record elusive bird songs and isolate the songs from surrounding noise.

The tools for analyzing bird song once it has been recorded also have become far more sophisticated in recent years. In earlier days, bird researchers and enthusiasts relied on musical notes to transcribe and compare songs. Now, computer-generated spectrograms can display visually all the details and shadings of a song so that individual songs can be put side by side for analysis.

Modern digital recordings can also be easily modified. By changing the order, frequency, or tempo of the various elements and playing the altered songs back to wild birds, scientists can determine which elements of the song are critical to transmitting its message.

Recorded bird songs and calls are used for more than purely scientific study. They can also be employed to influence the behavior of wild birds. Recordings of the alarm call of the herring gull, for example, have been used to repel flocks of gulls from garbage dumpsters.

Mimics

From buzzing chain saws to barnyard squeals, car horns to delicate piano concertos—it seems that there are precious few sounds that can't be mimicked by birds. However, while some species are capable of imitating a wide variety of noises, the most frequently mimicked sounds in the avian community are the songs of other birds.

The theories as to why certain birds mimic others are as varied as the imitations themselves. Some scientists believe that the imitators aren't really fooling anyone—even other birds. They are simply engaging in vocal appropriation to expand their repertoires, the better to scare off rivals and attract more mates. If this is the case, the marsh warbler must be a veritable Casanova. The bird has been found to imitate some two hundred European and African species. The songs that the male warbler picks up during its winter stay in Africa may also cue its potential mates as to what regions the suitor frequents, thereby attracting females that follow those same migratory patterns—a simple case of birds of a feather flocking together.

Other species seem to use their talent for mimicry as defense against predators. The thick-billed euphonia has perfected the mobbing calls of other species nesting nearby. When its nest is threatened, the euphonia raises its pilfered call to arms and the offending intruder is driven away by a swarm of duped neighbors. Like all good instigators, the euphonia can often be spotted surveying the ensuing melee from a safe distance.

For its part, the female burrowing owl can imitate the sound of a rattlesnake with blood-chilling accuracy. Discretion being the better part of valor, even the hungriest predator will bypass the owl's nest at the first sound of the fake rattle.

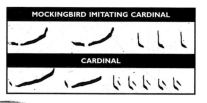

MOCKINGBIRD IMITATING CARDINAL

CARDINAL

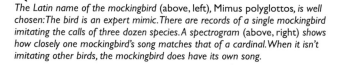

The Latin name of the mockingbird (above, left), Mimus polyglottos, is well chosen: The bird is an expert mimic. There are records of a single mockingbird imitating the calls of three dozen species. A spectrogram (above, right) shows how closely one mockingbird's song matches that of a cardinal. When it isn't imitating other birds, the mockingbird does have its own song.

Still other birds are known to use their vocal trickery to con other species into raising their young for them. Some experts speculate that the male indigo bird uses mimicry to lure a female of another species from its nest so that the female indigo bird can swoop into the vacated perch and lay its own egg alongside the others. Unaware of this sleight of wing, the host female will return to the nest to hatch the eggs and raise the counterfeit chick as its own.

Mynas are among the most popular of the domestic birds, largely because of their imitative vocal abilities.

Even the young take part in the deception. The koel, a cuckoo found in Africa and India, frequently lays its eggs in the nests of Indian crows. Young koels get their foster parents' attention by mimicking the begging sounds of their "siblings." Those koels that have not been raised by Indian crows do not include those distinctive sounds in their vocal repertoire.

Calling the Dog

There are many documented stories of the near flawless abilities of some birds to imitate nonavian sounds. In one study, a crested lark in Germany learned to mimic four different whistled commands that a shepherd used with his dog to tell it where to run and at what speed. When the lark's recorded impersonations were played, the dog obeyed the command correctly every time.

TALKING BIRDS

Among humans, the most popular form of bird mimicry is when pets are taught to talk. Mynahs, magpies, and even crows are the most adept at imitating human speech. Although some talented mimics do not understand what they are saying, others are capable of basic word association. Certain parrots have been known to greet people walking in the door with a raucous "hello," while others have been trained to whistle a piece of classical music at the mere mention of the title. And there is the case of Alex, the parrot that can correctly answer conceptual questions *(page 19)*.

BIRDS IN YOUR BACKYARD

THE WELL–EQUIPPED BIRDER

One of the enduring attractions of birdwatching is that it takes so little equipment to get started.

Enjoyable birding means first getting a good look at that bird flitting through the bush, and then identifying it. The first step requires a good pair of binoculars *(pages 80–81)*; the second, a reliable field guide.

CHOOSING A FIELD GUIDE

Scan the bookstore shelves and you'll be overwhelmed by the number of field guides on the market.

Most are designed to fit in a pocket or small bag, but of course there's a trade-off to be made between the number of birds covered and the amount of information provided on each one. Many guides cover all of North America, while others include only the birds of the East or West. If you happen to be in the middle of the continent, you'll have to choose a North American guide

Along with a trusty field guide, a notebook, and pencils, basic birding equipment includes sturdy hiking boots; a good jacket or vest with lots of pockets; a hat to shield you from the sun; binoculars; and a waist pouch or backpack.

> *"The naturalist accomplishes a great deal by patience, more perhaps than by activity."*
>
> — Henry David Thoreau

Roger Tory Peterson

Biologist, conservationist, painter, and nature photographer, Roger Tory Peterson was also the father of the modern field guide. Frustrated by the unwieldiness of existing guides, he found a way to present the essential information needed by a birder compactly enough to fit into a pocket. *Peterson's Field Guide to the Birds*, published in 1934, featured field marks for each bird—the distinguishing characteristics that help in identifying the species. Today, field guides are standard equipment for birders.

or carry one for both the East and West. There are also specialized guides for your specific state or region, other guides that cover only your favorite family of birds, such as hawks or hummingbirds, and still others on the birds of just about any foreign country you may choose to visit. In time you likely will accumulate a variety of guides, carrying a dog-eared favorite with you in the field and keeping the rest of your library at home or in the car for reference on that hard-to-identify bird.

Any guide you choose should have clear images of each bird, maps that show the ranges they appear in at different times of year, and easy-to-follow text that points out the field markings to look for and helps you distinguish among similar species. Guides that are easiest to use have all the information about each bird on the same page. Look also for one with color coding or some other system that allows you to flip quickly to the right family of birds. Some birders find that good-quality illustrations show the relevant field markings more clearly than photographs and are better at representing a bird that is typical of its species; however, guides with very sharp photographs can also be a good choice.

Once you've chosen a guide, take the time to read the introductory material explaining how the book is organized, and the terms and symbols that are used.

OTHER EQUIPMENT

Before heading out into the field, make sure you're comfortably dressed *(opposite)* and equipped with the basic supplies to enjoy the outdoors. And, of course, you'll need a convenient way to carry everything. Although many birders head out into the woods with little more than binoculars, field guide, and notebook, avid birders may find they want to invest in more specialized equipment such as spotting scopes, cameras with telephoto lenses, and tape recorders to spot and document their finds *(page 84)*.

Choosing and Using Binoculars

If you really want to watch birds, you'll need to improve your vision. Binoculars are the birder's mainstay. While this might be obvious, it gets a little more complicated when you're standing in a store before a case full of different makes and models. This is where your level of experience, individual needs, and budget come into play.

But first, you'll need a primer in optics. Binoculars come in different "prescriptions." These are expressed in numbers such as 7×35 and 10×40. The first number refers to the factor of enlargement over the naked eye. A pair of 7×35 binoculars magnifies an image seven times. The second number refers to the diameter, in millimeters, of the objective lenses—the ones at the front of the binoculars. So, now you're ready to buy the pair with the highest magnification and largest lens, right? Wrong.

There are important optical trade-offs to consider. High enlargement puts you up close, but this comes at the expense of something called field of view. Simply put: Your total picture is smaller. This makes it hard to find and keep up with fast-moving birds such as warblers and wrens. You also need a rock-steady hand because the larger image is sensitive to the smallest twitch.

Lens diameter also involves compromises. More light means a better image at dusk and a wider field of view. But it also means more weight. As a general rule

Birdwatchers once identified birds by shooting them in order to examine them up close. Today binoculars provide a more humane way of spectating and studying birds.

Porro-prism binoculars (below, left) tend to be heavier and bulkier than roof-prism binoculars (below, right), which feature a more elaborate system of light-refracting prisms that makes possible a lightweight, slim design. But that advantage in size and weight comes at a cost: Roof-prism types are usually more expensive.

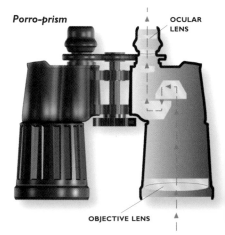

Porro-prism

OCULAR LENS

OBJECTIVE LENS

of thumb, you'll want to divide the lens diameter by the magnification factor and hope to arrive at a number no lower than five. The most popular binoculars lie between 7×35 and 10×50. When in the store, don't get carried away by magnification alone; you'll also want to view birds that are not so distant. Make sure you can focus on objects less than ten feet away, preferably between six and eight feet. Finally, try focusing on the cash register—without shaking.

TWO TYPES OF BINOCULARS

Binoculars come in two basic types: Porro- and roof-prism. Porro-prisms are the quintessential binoculars— the type you imagine a navy commander using to scan the horizon. Named after their Italian inventor, they feature four refractions—that is, interior mirrors bend incoming light four times. This, along with their large objective lenses, means that lots of light reaches your eye. Thus, they are good for low-light conditions. The large lenses also mean a wider field of view, and they

Quick Tips
- Practice spotting objects in your backyard and quickly sighting them through the binoculars before heading into the field.
- When you see a bird, keep watching it as you bring the binoculars up to your eyes to avoid losing sight of it.
- Use a neck strap. It keeps the binoculars close at hand and prevents them from being dropped.

give greater image dimension. But they can be heavy and bulky. Roof-prism binoculars bend light five times, bringing a little less light to your eye. But they usually are light and compact, making them more user-friendly in the field. Be wary of featherweights—high-quality glass is dense and somewhat weighty.

Whatever binoculars you choose, look for a center-focusing dial for quick focusing and a dioptric compression ring to help "fit" the binoculars to the differences between your left and right eyes. Also check the glass. All lenses should be coated with a glare-reducing agent such as magnesium fluoride. You can evaluate the coating by turning the ocular (eye-end) lens to the light and checking the reflection. Poor glass yields a yellow reflection, quality glass a blue or lavender reflection.

Finally, are the binoculars waterproof and dustproof? Do they have rubber eyecups? Take them out for a test. Is the focusing wheel easy to use, allowing you to zero in quickly on fast-moving birds? Last but not least, are they comfortable to handle?

Roof-prism

OCULAR LENS

OBJECTIVE LENS

Birding in the Field

For you, birding may mean anything from a solitary ramble along a country road to an organized group outing into the wilderness. Once you've decided where and when to take your excursion, getting the most out of your field trip means dressing appropriately, making sure you have a few basic supplies, and learning some simple tricks and techniques for seeing as many birds as possible.

PLANNING A FIELD TRIP

As you begin your search for birds, don't discount city parks and other urban areas such as abandoned railway tracks, cemeteries, and vacant lots. Moving farther afield, you can find birds in any of the habitats discussed on page 114, from the seashore to grasslands. Wildlife refuges are ideal choices. Birding can become an exciting focus to your travels as well, as you seek out some of the birding hot spots in North America *(page 170)*.

Birding can be satisfying at any time of year, but spring and fall migration periods are ideal times to see great numbers of birds. The best times of day to bird are early morning and a few hours before dusk, when birds are most active. Weather patterns also affect the birds you see. Bad weather can stall migrating birds, causing a "backup" in one spot. A local shower, though, may presage the unexpected treat of seeing birds emerge to sing and dry off in the sun.

WHAT TO WEAR

Dress for a birding trip in much the same way you would for any hike or walk. To avoid having your day spoiled by rain, you may want a rain jacket and pants. However, these impermeable suits can become hot and sweaty on a brisk walk. Gore-Tex outerwear, although expensive, is both waterproof and breathable. In a dry climate, you can get by with a lightweight windbreaker of breathable, quick-dry nylon.

Under your jacket, dress in light layers. Polypropylene long under-

---

> ## Some Birding DOs
>
> - Wear drab colors—camouflage clothing is not necessary—and avoid articles that rustle.
> - Speak softly and avoid sudden movements. Keep your binoculars always at-the-ready.
> - Try to stand with the sun at your back to make birds easier to spot and more visible.
> - Keep your eye on the bird for as long as possible, observing every detail you can, before consulting your field guide.

A great way to get more involved in your new hobby is to join your local birding club. You can learn from more experienced birders and join in trips to birding spots in your area.

wear will wick water away from your body, and wool socks over polypropylene ones will help your feet to stay warm even when wet. In areas with Lyme disease, wear long pants and a shirt with cuffs to keep ticks at bay.

For walking on roads and well-kept paths, running shoes are fine, but if you plan to be scrambling over rocks and logs, you'll want sturdy, lightweight hiking boots.

A broad-brimmed hat serves the dual purpose of keeping the sun off your face and preventing rain from running down your neck. Choose one that is well-ventilated and snug enough not to blow off in a strong wind. In cold weather, opt for a wool hat instead.

WHAT TO CARRY

You can carry your lunch, sunscreen, and insect repellent in a backpack. However, you will want to keep your guidebook, notepad, and pencils closer at hand. A waist pouch is perfect for this, and there are models for birders made with several pockets. Special vests or

Keeping a Record

Some birders are content to keep a journal of their field trips, including everything from notes on the weather and habitat to observations of bird behavior and sketches made with color pencils. But for many, keeping lists is an integral part of birding. A "life list" is a list of every species of bird you've seen during your birding career, sometimes restricted to a particular geographical region. You can make the list yourself or purchase a printed checklist. Lists are also available on CD-ROM. Variations on the life list include yard lists and year lists. Keep your records in pencil to prevent them from being ruined in the rain.

shirts are also available with pockets to suit just about any need.

Your binoculars can be kept around your neck, or in a pocket if they're small enough. A pair of light gloves makes handling them easier. And don't forget a lint-free cloth to wipe the lenses when they fog up.

If your main goal is to spot raptors, wear sunglasses to help you pick them out against a bright sky. You might even bring a folding chair for sitting when staking out a site. On any excursion, take plenty of water.

The Advanced Birder

Spotting scopes can pick up details of a bird a couple of hundred yards away. They are particularly useful for observing ducks and shorebirds.

Thanks to modern technology, the advanced birder can get closer to birds than ever before. Many bird-watchers now swear by spotting scopes. These can be a wonderful complement to binoculars, offering up greatly magnified images to the birder. Mounted on a sturdy tripod, the scope eliminates the shake associated with binoculars. A scope is perfect for viewing static scenes such as nests or perches, or even beaches humming with avian activity. It also frees up the hands for taking notes or unwrapping a candy bar.

Naturally, there are some minuses. Scopes are often long and heavy, and the associated tripods tend to be even longer and heavier. They are also ill-suited to keeping track of fast-flying birds, since their field of view is narrow. In certain conditions, their flat, telescoped image can accentuate visual disturbances such as heat waves and mirages, making birds hard to see. Then, too, one must choose between a fixed focal length or zoom mechanism. As with camera lenses, a zoom might seem to offer enhanced flexibility, allowing fingertip magnification changes. But taking advantage of this feature can be a vexing challenge in the field. In zoom lenses, magnification and focus are separate functions, and the split-second calibration of both can prove tricky. Alternatively, fixed-focal-length scopes allow you to change magnifying power by switching eyepieces. To zoom or to switch? It's really a matter of personal preference. Just make sure the scope has an erecting prism; otherwise, the image you see will be backwards and you will be forever panning in the wrong direction. Spotting scopes need not always be anchored onto a tripod. Special mounts now permit you to brace your scope on your shoulder or the window of your car, depending on your preferred viewing site.

PHOTOGRAPHING BIRDS

As long as you can see it, you can photograph it, right? Well, not necessarily. While photographing birds is deeply rewarding, there's more to the job than passing film behind a scope or pair of binoculars. This is

Photographing birds requires a good camera and telephoto lens—and a lot of patience.

a true art and a test of your understanding of bird behavior. Good bird photography isn't about gathering a collection of avian mug shots, but about illustrating the creature's relationship to its habitat, its climate, and its fellow birds. So, you need to have some knowledge about birds as well as cameras.

Only single-lens-reflex (SLR) cameras should be used for bird photography. SLRs allow you to change lenses—and you'll be doing lots of that. Bird photography requires stealth, patience, and really powerful lenses. You'll be using 300- to 800-millimeter lenses, and this means that you'll need a tripod since these lenses are too awkward and heavy to hold steady by hand.

Beyond technology lies the *art* of bird photography. Know what you are seeing and why it is worth photographing. Try to set the bird off against its background, either by color contrasts or by altering the depth-of-field or exposure time to blur the surroundings. Apply the "rule of thirds," placing the subject one-third of the way into the frame, facing or moving into the larger empty area. This will add a dynamic quality to your photographs and help bring them to life.

SOUND RECORDING

For many birders, a chirp is worth a thousand pictures. If you find bird songs interesting, you may want to invest in advanced audio gear. It's not just a fad—sounds are a key aspect of avian behavior and you can often learn more by listening than by watching. Today the market is filled with portable digital recorders and lightweight directional microphones that make capturing bird sounds as easy as pressing a button.

Whether viewing or listening in on the private lives of birds, remember that technology is no replacement for good birding skills. Patience, unobtrusiveness, and keen powers of observation are still the trademarks of the successful birder.

For sound recording, the microphone is as important as the recorder itself. Here, a birder uses a powerful directional mike to listen in on a bird song.

ATTRACTING BIRDS TO YOUR YARD

Dozens of species of birds can find an inviting home or way station in your backyard. All you have to do is make them feel welcome.

Whether they are squabbling at a feeder or carrying nesting material to a nearby tree, birds in your yard can provide you with viewing opportunities throughout the year—often from the indoor comfort of your home.

To make your yard an attractive habitat for birds, you'll need to offer them the same resources they would find in the wild: food, water, shelter, and nesting sites. These can be provided with feeders, birdbaths, and birdhouses, as described starting on page 90, but you can offer plenty of food sources and sheltered refuges with the trees, shrubs, and flowers you choose to plant.

This cedar waxwing has been tempted by a banquet of luscious red crabapples.

PLANNING A BIRD GARDEN

The most attractive garden for birds is not the traditional one with a close-cropped lawn and carefully tended flower beds. Birds like varied foliage, particularly "edge habitats," such as where woodlands give way to brush. You can reproduce this variety by planting your garden with tall trees, groups of shrubs, clambering vines, and small, open grassy areas, allowing each to blend into the next. The terrain itself can be varied with soil mounds, slopes, and rock gardens. Then, ease up on your pruning and weeding, and let it all go a little bit wild. Even an apartment balcony can be a welcome retreat for birds, landscaped with flower boxes and small potted trees and shrubs.

When you're choosing trees and plants for your garden, it's best to stick with local varieties that grow well in your area and will be familiar to visiting birds. A few suggestions are given in the chart on page 89, but it pays to consult your local horticultural society or botanical garden for advice on which plants are most successful in your region. Whatever you plant, do your avian visitors a favor and avoid using pesticides or herbicides.

PLANTS FOR SHELTER

Ideally your garden should provide birds with shelter from wind and rain, and offer them plenty of sites for nesting and raising their young. Many birds prefer a particular elevation for perching, nesting, or other activity. Chipping sparrows, for example, like to forage on the ground, nest in low shrubs, and sing from treetops. To attract the widest variety of birds to your garden, surround the base of tall trees with shorter trees and shade-loving shrubs or groundcovers.

Clusters of shrubs of different heights and kinds of foliage are particularly attractive to avian visitors. Dense growth provides the best nesting sites for many birds, so avoid over-pruning shrubs and trees. Dead branches and old tree stumps make your garden seem more like a wooded grove to birds; consider sacrificing a little neatness in order to encourage more birds.

Evergreen shrubs and trees offer essential shelter for birds that winter over in your area. Planting a row or hedge of them along the windward edge of your garden will also protect your entire property from bitter winter winds.

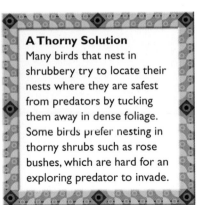

A Thorny Solution
Many birds that nest in shrubbery try to locate their nests where they are safest from predators by tucking them away in dense foliage. Some birds prefer nesting in thorny shrubs such as rose bushes, which are hard for an exploring predator to invade.

A large expanse of well-groomed lawn may please us aesthetically, but it offers the least appealing habitat to most birds, leaving them feeling exposed and vulnerable. Small areas of lawn will draw some birds out in the open where you can see them, but reserve corners of the lawn for tall grasses and weeds where the birds can flit for cover.

For birds to nest in your yard, they'll need to find not only an appropriate site, but also the materials to build their nests. Letting leaves and twigs fall where they may will offer a supply of nesting materials. Goldfinches will be pleased to collect fluff from weeds that have been left to go to seed.

PLANTS FOR FOOD

Which plants you choose will, of course, depend on the kind of birds you are trying to attract to your yard. Begin by finding out what birds are common in your area and what they prefer to eat.

Fruit-eating birds such as waxwings will be delighted with berry-producing shrubs and vines

A wide variety of shrubs and plants in this garden draws birds from the neighboring woodland.

choose plants that bear fruit at different times of year to keep the food supply continuous.

You can attract seed-eating birds such as finches and warblers by allowing perennials to go to seed—favorites are columbine, coreopsis, foxglove, California poppy, goldenrod, and sunflowers. And resist the temptation to eliminate weeds from your garden—dandelions and thistles also provide an excellent source of seeds. Certain trees such as maples are also a good source; see the chart opposite for suggestions.

planted for their benefit. They will also be pleased with any cherry trees they find, so you may want to plant extra ones to compensate for the fruit that you will inevitably lose. Favorite trees and shrubs are listed in the chart opposite; popular vines include honeysuckle, Virginia creeper, and grape. Some groundcovers also provide berries. Try to

To attract birds that dine on insects, let leaves and branches decay where they fall without raking them up—birds such as thrashers will scratch around under them to uncover grubs, earwigs, and other tasty treats. Most coniferous trees attract insects that birds can feed on. Watering any areas of lawn in dry weather will draw robins in search of earthworms.

This map, developed by the United States Department of Agriculture, divides the continent into eleven horticultural zones. The chart at right indicates the zones where the listed plants grow best.

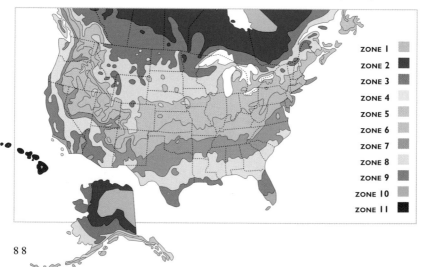

ZONE 1
ZONE 2
ZONE 3
ZONE 4
ZONE 5
ZONE 6
ZONE 7
ZONE 8
ZONE 9
ZONE 10
ZONE 11

TREES AND SHRUBS FOR ATTRACTING BIRDS

	PROVIDES	BIRD SPECIES	ZONES
TREE			
CHERRY	fruit	cardinals, finches, grosbeaks, jays, mockingbirds, robins, sparrows, thrashers, waxwings, woodpeckers	2-9
CRABAPPLE	fruit	bluebirds, cedar waxwings, flycatchers, grosbeaks, mockingbirds, robins, thrushes, vireos	2-6
HACKBERRY	fruit	bluebirds, cardinals, cedar waxwings, grosbeaks, mockingbirds, orioles, pigeons, robins, thrushes, woodpeckers	4-9
HAWTHORN	fruit, insects, seeds	cedar waxwings, grosbeaks, jays, mockingbirds, robins,	4-5
HEMLOCK	insects, seeds	chickadees, finches, grosbeaks, jays, kinglets, nuthatches, thrushes	3-7
MAPLE	fruit	finches, cedar waxwings, grosbeaks, orioles, robins, vireos, warblers	2-9
MOUNTAIN ASH	fruit	bluebirds, catbirds, cedar waxwings, grosbeaks, orioles, robins	3-7
MULBERRY	insects, fruit	bluebirds, cardinals, finches, grosbeaks, mockingbirds, robins, thrashers, towhees	4-9
OAK	nuts	chickadees, finches, grosbeaks, jays, nuthatches, orioles, owls, titmice, towhees, vireos, warblers, woodpeckers, wrens	2-11
SASSAFRAS	fruit	bluebirds, catbirds, robins, thrushes, vireos, woodpeckers	5-9
SERVICEBERRY	fruit	cedar waxwings, crows, grosbeaks, tanagers, thrushes, vireos, woodpeckers	3-8
WAX MYRTLE	fruit	cedar waxwings, flickers, robins, thrushes, towhees, warblers	7-8
SHRUB			
BAYBERRY	fruit	chickadees, finches, flickers, mockingbirds, robins, thrashers, thrushes, towhees	2-7
BRAMBLE (RASPBERRY, BLACKBERRY)	fruit	cardinals, catbirds, grosbeaks, mockingbirds, robins, sparrows, thrashers, vireos, warblers, wrens	4-10
DOGWOOD	fruit	bluebirds, cardinals, catbirds, grosbeaks, jays, robins, woodpeckers	3-8
ELDERBERRY	fruit	cardinals, cedar waxwings, flickers, grosbeaks, jays, mockingbirds	4-9
HOLLY	fruit	cardinals, cedar waxwings, mockingbirds, robins, thrashers, thrushes, towhees	3-9
SPICE BUSH	fruit, insects	bluebirds, cardinals, catbirds, flickers, mockingbirds, robins, thrushes	5-7
TOYON	fruit	cedar waxwings, flickers, grosbeaks, mockingbirds, robins, thrashers, thrushes, titmice, towhees	8-9
VIBURNUM	fruit, insects	bluebirds, cardinals, cedar waxwings, grosbeaks, mockingbirds, robins, sparrows, starlings, thrushes, towhees	4-11

Feeding Your Birds

Every year about one quarter of American households put out food for birds. Many limit the activity to winter, but feeding birds can be a rewarding year-round pastime.

HOPPER FEEDER

FEEDING THROUGH THE SEASONS

Winter feeding brings the largest number of birds to your feeder because natural food sources are scarcest then. Winter feeding doesn't have to mean always keeping your feeders full. Birds won't become entirely dependent on your feeders and will look elsewhere if they find them empty. Food you put out in winter, though, can help weak individuals through the bitter weather. Begin your winter feeding in the fall so the birds make your yard part of their routine before the cold sets in.

Feeding in spring and summer gives you an opportunity to observe birds in their mating and nesting periods. Don't worry about discouraging migratory birds from leaving on schedule—they'll depart when the hours of daylight begin to dwindle and the food you provide can strengthen them for their journey.

KINDS OF FOOD

The food you offer in your garden should provide the nutritional equivalent of the natural food sources preferred by each species. Determine which birds are common in your area, then consult the chart on page 177 for specific foods for each type. Make sure that whatever food you put out is fresh and free of mold.

Sunflower seeds will appeal to the largest number of seed-eating birds. Although expensive, black-oil sunflower seeds are the best choice; their thin shells are easiest to crack. Some bird species will eat sunflower seeds but prefer another type—niger seed is a favorite of goldfinches, siskins, and redpolls. If you offer a variety of seeds, put each type in a separate feeder; if you fill one feeder with a mixture, most birds will eat the desirable seeds and discard the rest. Seed-eaters also need a little grit to process seeds in the gizzard. In winter when exposed soil is scarce, put out a tray of chicken grit, which can be bought at farm supply stores.

Attract fruit-eating birds such as tanagers and orioles with raisins or other dried fruits softened with warm water. Alternatively, tap a nail into a fence post and impale a slice of a banana, orange, or apple on the nail. Feed orioles with sugar water put out in a commercial feeder or in a bottle used for hamsters; such bottles are available at pet stores.

Insect-eaters such as woodpeckers and nuthatches will eat seeds but are particularly drawn to suet placed in mesh bags or a log. Avoid suet when the temperature is warm enough to make the suet runny. If grease gets on the feathers, it can hamper flight. You can offer a peanut-butter mixture *(page 176)*, but keep it out of the sun. Meal worms are another favorite of insect-eaters, especially when nesting or caring for their young. In the spring, offer purple martins ground eggshells to replenish the calcium lost to egg creation.

A Gallery of Feeders

The versatile design of a hopper feeder (opposite) attracts ground- and perch-feeders. A window feeder (below) allows close-up observation—one-way glass prevents birds from being startled by indoor movements. Tube feeders (near right) are also popular, but don't appeal to ground-feeders; some models have dividers so more than one type of seed can be put out. Perchless globe feeders (far right) appeal to small clinging birds such as chickadees.

WINDOW FEEDER

FEEDERS

Feeding birds can be as simple as tossing a few handfuls of seed onto a walkway. A platform a couple of feet off the ground will keep fruit and scraps visible to passing birds and allow a number of species to feed together. To keep seeds clean and dry and to appeal to birds that don't like to feed on the ground, select one of the styles of commercial elevated feeders shown here, or make your own as described on page 178. The key to attracting a variety of species and preventing squabbles is to put the preferred food of each in a separate feeder. A vertical branch attached to the side of a feeder can provide extra perches.

Set your feeders where they are visible, preferably in a southeast corner where they will be warmed by the morning sun. If you are placing feeders near the house, put them within a few feet of windows; this way, if the birds are startled and fly toward the glass, they're less likely to build up enough speed to seriously injure themselves. If the seeds become damp, clean and disinfect the feeder with a solution of one part bleach to nine parts water.

TUBE FEEDER

GLOBE FEEDER

Dealing with Predators and Pests

If you live in a city or suburban area, birds are probably the only forms of wildlife that you see everyday. You can increase your birdwatching pleasure by installing feeders, birdhouses, and birdbaths. But take steps to protect these little outposts against attack.

The enemies of backyard birds are many and infinitely resourceful. They range from domestic and feral cats to nuisances such as squirrels and raccoons. Hawks, owls, and other raptors frequently raid nests and feeding stations. Fortunately, there are many steps you can take to assure that by attracting birds to your yard, you're not luring them to their deaths. Place feeders at least five feet off the ground and well away from shrubs and fences, beyond the range of leaping cats. Some birds will only come to

feeders put in trees or near bushes where they can take refuge at the approach of a predator. Try to accommodate this need without making it easy for the hunter. A little chicken-wire barrier at the base of a feeder will usually slow a cat long enough for birds to flee.

If you make life miserable for a feral feline, either by dousing it with water or beating on pans whenever it comes around, it will eventually move on to a less trying location. If you own a cat, you can help by keeping it indoors.

There's not much you can do if a hawk decides to drop by your feeding station for a breakfast of bird. You can try spooking it away, if you happen to catch it *in flagrante delicto*, but you may have to settle for reducing the amount of feed in the station to attract fewer birds.

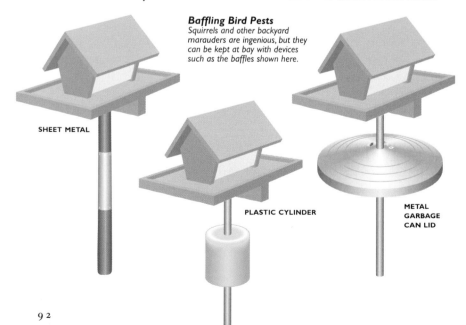

Baffling Bird Pests
Squirrels and other backyard marauders are ingenious, but they can be kept at bay with devices such as the baffles shown here.

SHEET METAL

PLASTIC CYLINDER

METAL GARBAGE CAN LID

FOILING SQUIRRELS

Squirrels are notorious feeder burglars. They can jump four feet from a standing start, climb around overhanging ledges, and perform highwire acts that rival the best circus shows. To prevent them from ascending post-mounted feeders, use squirrel baffles—cones or cylinders of metal or another slippery material that fit over feeder posts. You can make these yourself with aluminum flashing. Just be sure to mount baffles at least four feet off the ground. The same baffles work for raccoons, although you may want to consider a "stovepipe" style to thwart these strong and agile predators. These are made from stovepipe or polyvinyl chloride (PVC) pipe and are placed around the feeder posts in such a way that they stay up, but wobble, denying traction. Another solution is to mount feeders on steel poles coated with No. 10 motor oil.

Don't be fooled into thinking that feeders suspended on wires are safe from squirrels. You'll need to protect these, too. One good method is to feed the wire through a series of 35-mm film canisters. This not only prevents squirrels from reaching the feeder, but it also gives you the enjoyment of watching their devious raids turn into log-rolling contests that they can never win.

CUTTING DOWN ON TOXINS

Cats, hawks, and raccoons aren't the only threat to backyard birds. There are other slow, silent killers

A Squirrel-proof Feeder

The devious abilities of squirrels have spawned an entire industry of deterrents. In addition to baffles (*opposite*), there are feeders designed to thwart the cleverest of thieves. The model shown below closes up automatically when anything heavier than a bird lands on the perch.

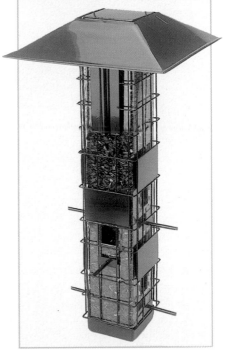

at work—toxic chemical pesticides and herbicides that find their way into the avian food chain. The best solution is to stop using them. Instead, consider devoting some areas of your yard to wildflowers and—yes—weeds. Poppies, cosmos, ragwort, nettle, and other wild species attract beneficial insects and birds, especially finches. The insects serve as a natural pesticide. And the finches eat flower seeds.

Jewels of the Garden

Darting from flower to flower, the sun glinting off their iridescent colors, hummingbirds seem the ultimate incarnation of ornithologist Roger Tory Peterson's claim that "birds are, perhaps, the most eloquent expression of

Bright-colored, trumpet-shaped flowers are popular magnets for hummingbirds.

reality." With the right flowers, feeder, and nectar solution, you can draw these dazzling aerialists to your yard.

PLANNING YOUR GARDEN

Hummingbirds' favorite blossoms are generally trumpet-shaped and colored with reds, pinks, oranges, and yellows; examples include columbines, fuschia, penstemons, and salvia. These plants have evolved in partnership with the hummingbird. The blossoms produce a glucose-rich nectar, which hummers need to fuel their demanding metabolism. The shape of the blossom allows greater room for nectar production and easy access for the hummingbird's bill. The blossom's color attracts the hummer, which picks up pollen on its head and breast as it feeds, then transfers the pollen to other blossoms, thereby assisting in crosspollination.

Homemade Nectar

Here's how to make your own hummingbird feeder nectar:
1. In a saucepan, combine one part white sugar with four parts water.
2. Boil briefly to dissolve the sugar and sterilize the solution.
3. Refrigerate the mixture.

Some DON'Ts to keep in mind:
• Don't make the mixture stronger than one-to-four. It can cause dehydration and possibly liver damage.
• Don't substitute honey, which can develop a mold that causes infections in hummers.
• Don't use artificial sweeteners. Hummingbirds drink nectar for the calories, which sweeteners lack.
• Don't boil the solution more than a few seconds or it can become too concentrated.
• Don't use artificial coloring. It has been linked to birth defects in hummingbirds.

Trumpet honeysuckle vines and morning glory also work well to attract hummingbirds, and their height makes it easier to observe the birds while they feed. Ideally, your garden should bloom for the entire period hummers are expected in your area. Plant a mix of species with different flowering times.

A HUMMINGBIRD FEEDER

If hummingbirds already visit your neighborhood, a feeder is a great way to attract them to your yard. A feeder works much like the flowers themselves, offering a glucose-rich nectar solution in a container designed for the hummingbird's feeding convenience. Hummingbirds tend to be loyal visitors: Once they find a feeder, they often come back every day throughout the season—and even year after year.

Start by hanging the feeder near blossoms that are visited by hummingbirds. Once the birds are using it, the feeder can be moved to another area of the yard where you can best watch and enjoy. Preferably, it should be out of direct sunlight (to keep the nectar solution fresher for longer) and sheltered from the wind. If bees and wasps seem to be drain-ing your feeder, coat the feeding areas with salad oil.

You'll want the feeder to be easily accessible for maintenance. Nectar solution ferments rapidly and must be changed frequently. (Fermented, cloudy solution still attracts hummers but may contain harmful bacteria or other unhealthy elements). Wash and refill the feeder every three days, using a toothbrush to scrub every cranny with a solution of dishwashing liquid and very hot water. Then rinse thoroughly.

The feeders that come apart completely and do not have any hard-to-get-at corners are the easiest to clean. Ideally, the feeder should have feeding ports facing up; the ones that face down tend to drip and attract insects. Feeders made of clear plastic make it easy to keep track of the times for refills. While most bright colors tend to attract hummingbirds, red is a perennial favorite.

Keep the feeder operating for the entire period that hummingbirds are expected and for several weeks after the last hummingbird is seen. You may have the odd migrant passing through.

Hummingbird feeders come in a wide array of shapes and colors. You can use a commercial model like the one shown or fashion your own from a hamster water bottle. The feeder should be decorated in red to provide maximum attraction: Red nail polish or red ribbons work well.

Birdbaths and Ponds

The setting is pure Victorian. At the center of a manicured expanse of lawn stands a steep-sloped birdbath on a white Grecian pedestal. One problem, though: no birds. Yet less than a hundred feet away, two magnolia warblers splash excitedly in the shallow puddle of a discarded pie plate.

As aesthetically pleasing as the Victorian birdbath may be to humans, it is judged with a more critical eye by the birds it was designed to attract. From their vantage point, this is a dangerous place to take a dip.

To begin with, many birds have a healthy fear of deep water. Birdbaths that drop suddenly to depths of more

Bathing is more than just a pleasure activity for birds. In summer it helps cool them, while regular dips in winter enable them to fight the cold by improving their feathers' ability to insulate.

Birdbaths in Winter

Winter can be an unforgiving season for birds in northern climates. A deep freeze denies birds water for drinking and preening. Keeping your birdbath operational through the chill of winter takes only a small initial investment. Submersible heaters, ranging from low-priced flat-coil types to high-tech devices with built-in thermostats, are available at specialty bird supply stores. Check the water level every few days. Once the water evaporates, a heater is at risk of burning itself out. And don't run the heater at all during a spell of sub-zero weather. Birds shouldn't be enticed to the warmed water to bathe if there is any chance that their feathers may ice up.

than three or four inches can be hazardous to small birds, especially to their young. Ideally your birdbath should have a gentle incline that provides birds with secure footing. Avoid baths with slick surfaces such as plastic; instead, opt for the type of roughened bottom found in cast stone. Don't fret a lot about cost; if expense is a consideration you can make a perfectly serviceable birdbath from the top of a metal garbage can.

LOCATION AND MAINTENANCE

Birds bathe not only to beat the summer heat. They also use the opportunity to preen themselves and keep their plumage in top flight condition. But a wet bird is a vulnerable bird. It needs a secure place to dry its feathers before it is able to fly well. Without the cover of nearby bushes or shrubs, small birds are the quintessential sitting ducks for predators—hawks and other raptors from above, as well as cats and other foes below.

Don't place your birdbath right beside bushes or directly under trees. Shrubs should be close enough to provide birds with a safe haven to dry and preen, but not so close that they become the beachheads for hungry cats. As for overhanging trees, falling leaves and debris will quickly dirty the water and have you bemoaning each gust of wind.

One surefire way to turn your quiet birdbath into a popular watering hole is the addition of a water drip. The sound of burbling water and the sight of ripples on the surface seem to have some sort of Pied-Piper effect on birds. A store-bought spout or miniature fountain is inexpensive and easy to install. You can also fashion your own simple drip bath from a metal pail, as shown at right.

Of course, the more popular your birdbath becomes, the more attention you'll have to pay to keeping it clean. Because birds will drink and bathe in the water, avoid chemicals and cleaning solvents. Just scrub the bath regularly to keep it algae-free.

A POND FOR YOUR BIRDS

If you have the space and the inclination, consider creating a small pond. Place it far enough away from bird feeders so debris doesn't fall in, but close enough to your garden hose to make cleaning simple.

As with a birdbath, the most important aspects of your pond are the pitch of its slope and the depth of water. Make sure that you dig the grade so it drops gradually from the edge. In large pools, partially submerged rocks make perfect perches for thirsty birds.

Excavating a site and constructing even a small pond can be an involved process. After digging the hole, you should line the bottom with wire mesh and several inches of sand, followed by a waterproof liner, available at garden centers, so your little oasis is watertight. For a more elaborate pond, add a water drip, fountain, waterfall, and a circulation pump.

A Simple Drip Bath
You can make your own drip bath from a twelve-quart metal pail. Drill a small hole and increase it in size until it emits from twenty to thirty drips per minute. Cover the pail to keep out insects and leaves.

97

Birdhouses

A stocked bird feeder will invite birds to stop by for a meal, but a nest box will encourage them to move into your backyard and stay for a few months. With their pruned landscapes, urban areas often suffer from a shortage of suitable nesting sites. Birdhouses provide an opportunity for you and your family to observe avian visitors raising their young.

Birds that nest in cavities in the wild prefer enclosed nest boxes, while other species are drawn to a simple shelf. In either case, put up the house as early as January—birds that don't migrate often start to scout for nesting sites in the depths of winter. Don't be disappointed if no one moves in soon—some species will keep an eye on a box for a couple of years before accepting it as part of the landscape.

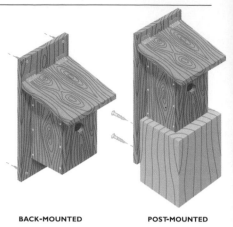

BACK-MOUNTED   **POST-MOUNTED**

MATERIALS

Both nest boxes and shelves should be made of materials that weather well. Cedar and redwood are naturally resistant to rot and insects, but less expensive woods such as pine will still last a number of years. Make sure that any glue you use is exterior grade and that nails or screws are galvanized to avoid rust.

There's no need to sand the wood you use—rough-cut lumber appeals to most birds. Leave the inside surfaces unfinished since many stains and paints can be toxic. You can leave the outside unfinished as well and let the wood weather to a natural gray. If you want to stain or paint the house, choose a light earthy color. Dark colors can turn your birdhouse into a sweat box.

Back from the Brink

Bluebirds are cavity nesters that take over unused woodpecker holes. The destruction of woodlands as well as competition from two European species—house sparrows and starlings—almost wiped out the species in this century. Over the last few decades, an army of volunteers has been creating "bluebird trails"— networks of regularly monitored boxes on farmland and along country roads. These efforts have restored bluebird numbers. For information on building and monitoring your own bluebird boxes, contact your local bluebird society.

**PIPE-MOUNTED
WITH FLANGE**

**PIPE-MOUNTED
WITH CLAMPS**

Box Mounting Methods
*Nest boxes can be attached by extending the back
of the box and nailing through it or by setting the box
on a post and allowing the back to extend down it.
To discourage predators, consider mounting the box
on a metal pole. Gas pipes work well and can be
driven into the ground easily. Attach the box to the
pole with a pipe flange fastened to the bottom of
the box or with clamps secured to the back.*

Mount your nest box or platform
in a sheltered part of your yard
using any of the methods shown
opposite and above, and make sure
that you protect it from predators
(pages 92-93).

NEST BOXES

A wide variety of bird species
make their homes in natural cavities
such as holes in tree trunks. Many
species—such as chickadees, nuthatches, and tree swallows—will
be equally pleased to nest in a box
you construct for them in your yard.
Other species, such as kestrels,
screech owls, and even wood ducks,
will nest in boxes put up in the wild.

The dimensions of the box, the
size of the opening, and the height
of the box off the ground should be
tailored to the preferences
of the species of bird you're
trying to attract. A typical
plan along with the specific
requirements for a number
of different species are
given on page 179. If you're
trying to attract small birds,
limit the opening to less
than one and one-half
inches so that starlings
cannot take over the box.

Whatever design you
choose for your nest box,
it should incorporate certain basic
features. To keep the box snug and
dry, make sure the roof extends at
least three inches beyond the front
of the box, and add three-eighths-
inch drainage holes in the bottom
corners of the box. Small holes near
the top of the box sides will promote ventilation and keep the box
from appearing pitch black when a
bird sticks its head in the opening
for an inspection. To allow you to
take a peek at what's going on
inside and to clean the box, fit one
side with a hinge. There's no need
to add a perch to your birdhouse—
it will only invite house sparrows.
All cavity nesters have feet strong
enough to cling to the outside of
the house. However, fledglings can
sometimes have trouble climbing
out—a piece of lightweight metal
mesh, known as hardware cloth,
attached to the inside of the front
wall just below the opening will
make their job easier.

As a final touch, add a couple
of handfuls of wood chips (don't

Birdhouses don't have to be conventional in shape or material. Here, a Carolina wren checks out a wall-mounted jug as a possible nesting site.

use sawdust; it will tend to get soggy). Some birds will use the chips as a base for their nests, while others will be content with the chips alone as nesting material.

SHELVES AND PLATFORMS

Many birds are not cavity nesters in the wild, preferring to nest in thick grasses or the crotch of a branch. To attract birds such as robins and phoebes and keep them out of rain gutters, attach a nesting shelf to the side of a building or fence. You can build the shelf with sides and a roof, but leave the front open.

Some birds have very specialized preferences for nesting sites. You can attract mourning doves with a small cone of hardware cloth hung in the crotch of a tree.

KEEPING WATCH

One of the pleasures of putting up nest boxes and shelves in your yard is being able to watch the birds

coming and going with nesting material, and later with food for their nestlings. However, resist peeking into the box itself when the parent is building its nest or incubating its eggs—disturbing the parent at this point can cause it to abandon the box. Once you see the parent making frequent trips to the box with food, it's safe to assume the nestlings have hatched. At this stage, you can look into the box once or twice. Talk loudly as you

Bird Condos

Purple martins have long been prized for their insect-eating abilities and their iridescent purple plumage. They are also the only North American bird that will nest together in houses—in colonies of up to a hundred individuals. Native Americans placed hollowed out gourds near their homes as nesting sites for the birds, and over the centuries purple martins have abandoned natural nesting sites and become increasingly dependent on ones provided by their

To encourage birds to set up house in your yard, provide them with appropriate nesting materials by hanging a mesh bag filled with cotton balls, pet fur, hair clippings, and lengths of yarn or string a maximum of two inches long.

approach to warn the parent and give it a chance to leave. Limit your visit to about thirty seconds—long enough to note the construction of the nest and the number of nestlings for your records.

MAINTAINING THE BOX
Conventional wisdom holds that nest boxes should be cleaned out between seasons to remove unhatched eggs as well as mouse nests that may have been built during the winter. But recent research indicates that this may also remove the larvae of parasitoid wasps—insects that eat harmful parasites. In a natural cavity, the nesting material would be left in place, and you may want to treat nest boxes in the same way. If you do decide to clean out the boxes, do so in late winter. If, during the spring or summer, you noticed that the nestlings were infested with

mites—which in appearance are much like moving pepper grains—you can spray the empty box with a pyrethrin-based insecticide.

In the event that house sparrows or starlings have taken up residence in your nest box, you may want to evict them in favor of another local species. If you repeatedly remove their nesting materials as they try to build, the house sparrows will eventually give up and look for a more peaceful site elsewhere.

human hosts. Before you consider buying or building a purple martin house for your backyard, make sure that the species resides in your area *(page 145)*. In choosing a commercial house or making your own, make sure that it is lightweight so that it can be safely raised and lowered and that it is light-colored to avoid overheating. The house should accommodate at least eight families and conform with the dimensions given on page 179.

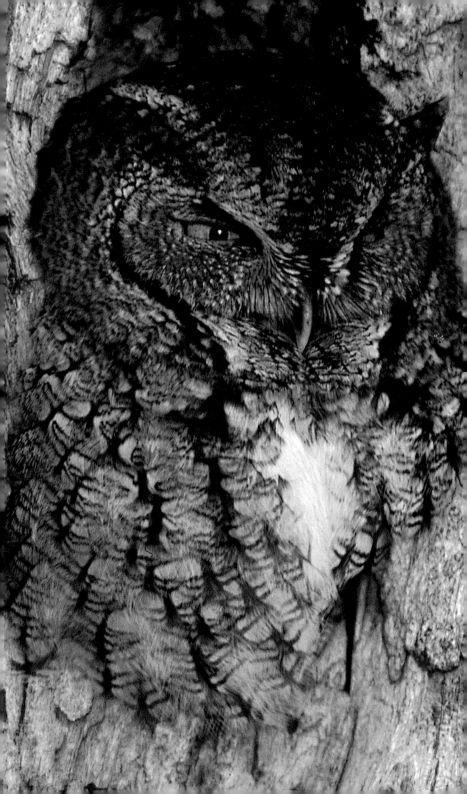

IDENTIFYING
BIRDS

BIRDS AT A GLANCE

With more than 9,000 bird species in the world, including 914 in North America alone, the only way to keep track is to group the species into meaningful categories.

As you are learning to identify birds, you will invariably find yourself trying to organize them by groups—all those with long beaks, for instance, those with broad wings and tails that soar, or all those you spot at the seashore. Scientists have found that the most useful system of categorization, or taxonomy, for learning about birds is one based on how closely they are related in the evolutionary tree.

> *"Hast thou named all the birds without a gun?"*
>
> — Ralph Waldo Emerson
> *Forbearance*

In other words, if you trace two bird species back to a common ancestor, are they siblings or merely distant cousins?

In modern bird taxonomy, each bird belongs to a distinct species—typically, individuals of different species cannot usually interbreed and produce fertile offspring. Species then are grouped with very similar ones into a genus. These genera are further sorted into fami-

Common and Latin Names

Common names for birds are often a poor indication of how closely related they are. The robin of North America, for example, belongs to a completely different family than the European bird of the same name. In 1758 the Swedish botanist Carolus Linnaeus developed a Latin naming system for plants and animals that would eliminate the confusion and allow scientists from all languages and cultures to communicate with each other.

In this system, each bird has a two-part name. The first part indicates the genus and the second, the species. So, for example, the blue jay is named *Cyanocitta cristata*. It shares the genus name *Cyanocitta* with other jays, but it alone is identified as *cristata*. Sometimes a third name indicating a sub-

species is added. For example, yellow-shafted flickers, which live east of the Rockies, are known as *Colaptes auratus auratus*, while red-shafted flickers west of the Rockies are *Colaptes auratus cafer*.

Both Latin and common names of birds often refer to the name of the person who discovered the species, to a prominent feature that distinguishes the birds' appearance or behavior, or to the place that has some association with the birds. John James Audubon, for example, named a warbler after his friend, the Reverend Bachman; the indigo bunting is instantly recognizable by its rich blue hue; and the first Cape May warbler known to ornithology was observed in Cape May, New Jersey.

lies, and families into orders. So, for example, the blue jay is grouped with other species of jays into the genus *Cyanocitta*, then into the family *Corvidae*, which also includes magpies and crows, then into the large order of *Passeriformes*, which includes all of the perching birds. And finally, all orders belong to the grand class *Aves*.

Taxonomy is not a simple science, however, and there is often debate about where to place a particular bird in the hierarchy. When deciding how to classify each kind of bird, ornithologists consider many factors—everything from the shape of the skull or the arrangement of the wing feathers right down to the composition of the blood plasma.

Sometimes two populations of birds long considered as separate species are discovered to belong to a single one. New evidence can even convince ornithologists to move a species from one genus to another. Modern DNA sequencing techniques are helping scientists solve many puzzles by allowing them to directly "read" and compare the genetic material of two individual birds.

Grouping birds based on an evolutionary hierarchy can lead to some surprising results. Loons, for example, are similar in shape to ducks, but belong to a completely different order. Most comprehensive field guides group bird species by family and order. However, since similar-looking birds do not necessarily belong

Order Out of Complexity

Traditional field guides often present bird families in the same sequence. The reason may not seem obvious. Why start with the reclusive loon and leave to the end the sparrows that fill a yard? In general, the arrangement is based on how old the particular order or family is considered to be—that is, how early it branched off in the evolutionary tree. Loons are believed to belong to the oldest order, while *Passeriformes*, the large order to which sparrows belong, has evolved most recently.

In some field guides, penguins are presented first because it was believed that they belonged to a very old order that had not yet evolved the ability to fly. It is now known that the oldest ancestors of birds did in fact fly and that flightless birds such as penguins have since lost the ability.

to the same family, this grouping system can appear bewildering when you first begin observing and identifying birds.

The identification guide section of this book *(pages 118-169)* groups birds according to the first thing a birder will probably notice about them—their general shape or silhouette *(pages 106-107)*. In some cases, as with the category called Gulls and Terns, all members belong to a single family. In other categories, such as Hawk-shaped Birds, the members belong to a single order. In still other cases, Duck-shaped Birds (which includes loons), for instance, a category may group more than one order of birds.

Bird Silhouettes

SEABIRDS These large coastal birds, such as gannets and puffins, spend most of their time in the water or squatting on the shore, often in large groups. Because their feet are located far back on their bodies, you will see them sitting almost upright.

SMALL WADERS Most members of this group, such as sandpipers and plovers, can be seen scurrying along the shore foraging with their slender beaks. Killdeers, which are of a similar shape, live inland.

LONG-LEGGED WADING BIRDS Conspicuous for their stilt-like legs, large birds such as cranes and herons often can be spotted wading in shallow water—some species in coastal areas and others in lakes and streams.

DUCK-SHAPED BIRDS While some species are familiar to everyone, ducks exist in an astonishing variety. They are seen most often swimming in lakes and rivers, but also inhabit salt water. Grebes and loons, although of different orders, are similar in shape.

GULLS AND TERNS Both gulls and their close cousins, terns, spend most of their time soaring above water. They are medium-sized and have long pointed wings. Although associated with the sea coast, these birds can be seen virtually anywhere on the continent.

HAWK-SHAPED BIRDS Also called birds of prey, these birds can most often be spotted soaring overhead or perched high in trees or on telephone poles or wires. All have sharp talons and hooked beaks for grabbing and tearing prey. They range in size from the 10.5-inch-long American kestrel to the 36-inch-long bald eagle.

OWL-SHAPED BIRDS
With their large round faces and soft-looking plumage, these birds are recognizable to all and difficult to confuse with any other kind of bird. Some, but not all, have visible ear tufts. Most are nocturnal hunters; during the day they may be spotted roosting in trees.

CHICKEN-SHAPED BIRDS
These birds, also known as game birds, include grouse and pheasants, and are similar in shape to the domestic chicken. They spend most of the time on the ground, camouflaged in the surroundings, but will flush up into the air if surprised.

PIGEON-SHAPED BIRDS
The pigeon, a familiar urban pest, is technically called a rock dove. Its cousin, the mourning dove, is its most common relative in the wild.

CLIMBING BIRDS
Woodpeckers can most often be spotted clinging to the side of a tree and balancing with their long tails. Brown creepers and nuthatches, also included in this category, are smaller and differ a bit in shape, but are also most often seen scurrying up or—in the case of nuthatches—down a trunk.

SWALLOW-SHAPED BIRDS
These graceful birds with pointed wings spend most of their time in the air, typically in large flocks. Purple martins, despite what their common name suggests, actually are a type of swallow.

PERCHING BIRDS
This is group includes the enormous order of *passeriformes,* or passerines. These birds, from finches to ravens, all have one toe pointing backwards to grasp branches. Hummingbirds and kingfishers, although unrelated, are grouped here because of their similar silhouette.

Narrowing Down the Choices

On a woodland walk, you spot a bird clinging to the side of a tree. From its shape and perch you can tell that the bird is some kind of woodpecker. Pulling out your binoculars, you watch for a few minutes. Soon, the bird is on the ground, probing what looks like an anthill—not typical woodpecker behavior. Eventually, you hear its call, "Wicka-wicka-wicka," as it flies off in an undulating way, revealing a white patch on its rump as it vanishes in the distance.

You jot down a few observations in your notebook, then consult your field guide to find that the bird's call, flight, feeding behavior, and markings identify it as a common flicker. If you had a chance to notice its black mustache you would even be able to identify it as a male; a red patch on the nape would tell you it belonged to an eastern subspecies.

Identifying birds often involves this kind of thorough detective work, observing not only the bird's appearance but also its behavior and song. For one bird, flight pattern alone may suffice for identification; for another, just the shape of its bill tells the tale. The important thing is to observe all you can while the bird is in view, keeping the following points in mind.

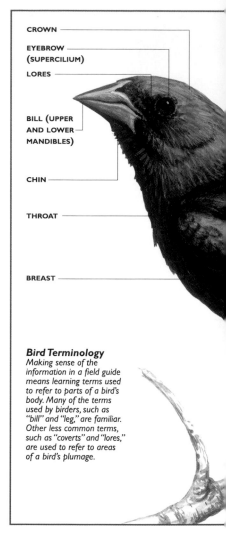

CROWN

EYEBROW (SUPERCILIUM)

LORES

BILL (UPPER AND LOWER MANDIBLES)

CHIN

THROAT

BREAST

Bird Terminology
Making sense of the information in a field guide means learning terms used to refer to parts of a bird's body. Many of the terms used by birders, such as "bill" and "leg," are familiar. Other less common terms, such as "coverts" and "lores," are used to refer to areas of a bird's plumage.

SHAPE

One of your first impressions of a bird's appearance is its overall shape. This can often lead you to the appropriate family of birds in your field guide or, in the case of this book, the group of birds with a shared silhouette *(pages 106-107)*. More detailed observations of the bird's shape may help you narrow down the choices. For example, although sandpipers all share a

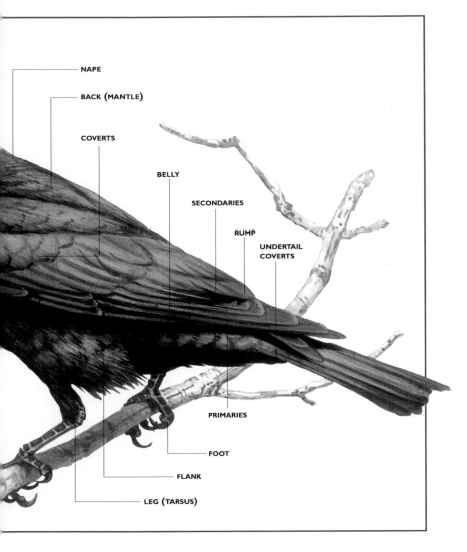

NAPE

BACK (MANTLE)

COVERTS

BELLY

SECONDARIES

RUMP

UNDERTAIL COVERTS

PRIMARIES

FOOT

FLANK

LEG (TARSUS)

similar silhouette, some have slender necks while others look like they have their heads hunched down on their shoulders. The bird's proportions—such as how far back on the tail the folded wings of a hawk reach—can also be a clue.

SIZE

Most field guides give you the size of each bird, measured from the tip of the bill to the end of the tail. Of course, in the field, the exact size of a bird is almost impossible to judge. A useful technique is to learn the sizes of a few familiar birds such as a sparrow, a robin, and a crow. You can then compare the bird you see with these "reference birds" and ask, "Is it bigger than a robin?" or "Is it smaller than a crow?" Sometimes the bird you are trying to identify will be surrounded by a flock of more familiar ones. In this case, the surrounding birds can serve as a size reference.

LOCATION

Simply noting where you spot a bird can eliminate countless possibilities. Water and land provide the most obvious differentiation: You are not going to see a loon perched in a tree or a sparrow swimming in a pond. Many field guides list water and land birds in separate sections, so this single observation can allow you to skip over a whole section. Next, consider the specific habitat in which you find the bird *(pages 114-115)*. A hawklike bird nesting on a recessed ledge of a downtown office building is most probably a peregrine falcon—not a northern harrier, which would more likely be spotted in open marshland.

The tail-wagging of this bird is a dead giveaway. It's typical behavior for a phoebe.

Finally, even within a particular habitat, birds have their favorite niches. Chestnut-sided warblers will usually be found flitting among the middle and outer branches of a tree, while yellow-rumped warblers are more likely to be spotted quite low in the tree or even on the ground.

In addition to noting the habitat, don't forget to consider where you are geographically. If it's

CROW   ROBIN   HOUSE SPARROW

Familiar birds can serve as reference points in judging the size of an unknown one. A house sparrow at six inches, a robin at ten inches, and a crow at twenty inches are good choices.

January in Michigan, and you suspect you may have seen a house wren, check your field guide for its winter range. Discovering that the bird is very rarely seen north of Kentucky at this time of year will tell you that you have to look for other possibilities.

BEHAVIOR

Don't just consider what your anonymous bird looks like—also observe what it is doing. Many birds have distinctive behaviors that are easy to recognize. Coots swim with a comical bobbing of their heads, while ruby-crowned kinglets constantly twitch their wings. And a nuthatch is the only bird you're likely to observe steadily winding its way down a tree trunk head-first.

Behavior traits can be particularly useful in telling apart birds that look physically similar at first glance. Some ducks, for example, dive completely beneath the water to snag their food while others dabble head-down with their rumps up.

Whether the bird is alone or in a group can be an important clue. Song sparrows, for example are loners and you're likely to see them singing on a solitary perch, while white-throated sparrows are seldom far from their flock.

Brown pelicans can be spotted taking a sudden dive into the water from heights of as much as thirty feet.

FLIGHT PATTERN

The manner of a bird's flight—whether the hovering of an American kestrel or the sudden dive of a kingfisher—can often tell you immediately what species you're looking at, or at least what family the bird belongs to. In some cases, just the shape of the bird in the sky is an important clue. For example, turkey vultures fly with their wings slightly raised, while black vultures keep them level with their body.

FIELD MARKS

Details of a bird's plumage and other distinguishing features such as the shape of the bill or the length of the legs are referred to as field marks and are some of the main clues provided in field guides. As you observe a bird, study it carefully from head to tail and note anything distinctive you see—from a splash of white on the tail to a bright yellow bill. Eyes, wings, and tails are areas that frequently carry special markings.

Often, a field mark is just one more clue to add to all the others, but sometimes a subtle distinction can really clinch the identification. For example, a woodpecker with a long beak—as long as its head—is a hairy woodpecker, not a downy woodpecker. A spotted thrush with rust coloring on its head is a wood thrush—but if the coloring is only evident on the tail, you've seen a hermit thrush.

As you try to match the field marks you've noted with those in your guide, keep in mind that a bird's markings may vary greatly, depending on the bird's age, its sex, and what point it is at in its molting cycle. A scarlet tanager matches its name only when wearing its breeding plumage. Most field guides will illustrate the differences between male, female, and juvenile birds, as well as their summer and winter plumage.

The names of birds might lead you astray in looking for field markings. Bird names often date back to many years ago when the creatures were killed and then examined in the hand for identification and naming purposes. For example, the red on a red-bellied woodpecker is carried very low on the belly—between the legs,

in fact—and is almost never visible to birders observing in the field.

BIRD SONG

In trying to identify that mystery bird, put your ears to work as well as your eyes. Some birds produce complete songs and others distinctive short calls *(pages 70-73).* In the case of the fifty species of closely related wood warblers, songs are often more distinctive than plumage—especially in the fall, when many of the the birds look

Eye Markings
Many small song-birds can be distinguished by markings around the eyes—the eyeline of a red-breasted nuthatch (right, top), the eye ring of a blue-gray gnatcatcher (right, bottom), and the eyebrow stripes of a red-eyed vireo (below).

like olive-brownish versions of the same bird. Flycatchers are so similar in appearance that differences in song are about all you have to go on to make the right identification. And at night, the call of a passing owl may be all the information about the bird that you manage to receive.

Field guides generally give some description of a bird's song, but the trick is to hold the song in your mind long enough to consult the

a song may remind you of some other sound such as the "squeaky-wheel" noise emitted by the black and white warbler.

Learning bird songs is one of the challenges and pleasures of birding. It's a good idea to begin by learning the songs of familiar backyard birds. With practice, your ears will even-

Tail Markings
Markings on the tail may be visible when a bird is at rest or flies off. They include the deep fork in the tail of a barn swallow (top left), the tail patch of an eastern towhee (left), and the bald eagle's all-white tail (below).

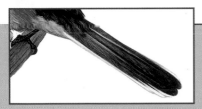

Wing Markings
The wings of birds often feature an area of contrasting color, such as the tips of a cedar waxwing (left), the patch of a red-winged blackbird (right), or the stripe or bar of a brown thrasher (below).

guide. Try whistling an imitation, then find some way of noting it on paper. Sometimes you can compare a bird's song to a phrase that matches its sound and rhythm, such as "Sweet, sweet, I'm so sweet," for a yellow warbler. Or,

tually be able to resolve a riot of bird song in the woods into the songs of individuals. Recordings are available to help you become familiar with common songs and at the same time bring a little bit of nature into your home.

Bird Habitats

Many of the smaller gulls look very similar, but if you see one perched on a telephone pole in the middle of open grassland, it's most likely a ring-billed gull. In identifying an unknown bird, knowing where each species is usually found can help you narrow the choices. In the Identification Guide *(pages 118-169)*, the preferred habitat of each bird is indicated with an icon like the ones shown on these pages. Of course, many birds will be equally at home in more than one habitat, such as both seashores and lakes and rivers. Some species are found throughout a wide range of habitats. In addition, a bird will sometimes stray from its usual home and settle into a completely different one. So when you head out on a field trip, be prepared for the occasional surprise.

FORESTS

Many species favor extensive treed areas with a closed canopy overhead. Some prefer to be high up in the canopy, others deep in the foliage, and still others in the underbrush. Certain species prefer either coniferous or deciduous forest. Forest birds are often easiest to spot where the forest gives way to more open areas.

WOODLANDS

Woodland areas are less dense than forest, less extensive, and have an open canopy overhead. Bird species that inhabit woodlands are often at home in city parks, small woodlots on agricultural land, and well-treed backyards. Some species will make their nests in trees, but prefer to forage in open areas nearby.

GRASSLANDS

There are many kinds of open grassland areas in North America: surviving native grasslands on the Great Plains, alpine meadows, tundra, and agricultural land. Grassland birds are often spotted on fence posts, on telephone wires, and amid roadside vegetation. Small clumps of trees will attract additional species.

DESERTS

Seemingly inhospitable, deserts are home to birds that have adapted to sparse rainfall—typically less than ten inches a year—and minimal vegetation. Areas range from the American Southwest to British Columbia, Canada.

INLAND CLIFFS

Many birds of prey are most at home on sheer-faced inland mountains. The birds use the cliffs as nesting sites and patrol nearby open areas for prey. Some birds of prey find that downtown office buildings can substitute for cliff faces.

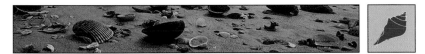

SEASHORES

Some bird species can be spotted cruising the coast line, others only far offshore. Still others forage in the mudflats formed at river estuaries. Coastal birds congregate on rocks or beaches, while seaside cliffs are home to huge numbers of colonial birds.

LAKES AND RIVERS

Some freshwater bird species spend their time out in deep water, while others wade in the shallows and still others prefer the muddy areas along the water's edge. Deep water often draws ducks that dive for their food, as well as loons and grebes.

WETLANDS

Marshy habitat areas range from prairie sloughs to mangrove swamps. Many bird species make their homes among the reeds, feeding on the plentiful insects.

Birds on the Run

With its massive ten-foot wingspan, the critically endangered California condor is one of the most impressive birds on the planet.

In 1962 Rachel Carson published *Silent Spring*, a milestone in environmentalism. Her title was inspired by the bleak prospect of a world without birds. Carson's words still resonate.

At last count, some eleven hundred bird species were acutely threatened—nearly 11 percent of all birds. When projections are adjusted to take into account all risk factors, nearly one-fifth of all birds are in trouble.

The International Union for the Conservation of Nature (IUCN) divides the most threatened species into three major categories: Critically endangered birds, currently numbering nearly one hundred species, which at current rates of decline have a 50 percent chance of becoming extinct within the next five years; endangered species, some two hundred, which run a 20 percent risk of extinction within twenty years; and vulnerable birds, four hundred or so species, which face extinction within the next century.

Habitat loss accounts for more than half of the problem. As human population grows, the number of birds dwindles. In the northern hemisphere, human encroachment on land, especially wetlands, robs birds of contiguous habitat, breeding and nesting areas, and stopovers along flyways. In the southern hemisphere, massive deforestation threatens to obliterate the core of the planet's terrestrial biodiversity, of which birds are a key component. When a forest disappears, birds lose shelter, food, and the fabric of social interactions on which their existence depends.

In both hemispheres, pollution plays a major role in population decline. In the 1960s, the pesticide DDT was blamed for widespread reproductive failure, particularly of birds sharing the food chain with humans. DDT was outlawed in the United States in 1972, but is still widely used in the rest of the world. DDT substitutes are proving to be just as harmful to birds, claiming at least 10 percent—some sixty-seven million—of the birds in the United States annually.

A TALE OF THREE BIRDS

Several species have been pulled back from the brink of extinction by a mix-

There are only about 4,500 piping plovers left in the world. Aggressive attempts to preserve its habitat may yet save the shorebird, currently classified as vulnerable by the International Union for the Conservation of Nature.

ture of science and social concern. The California condor was a victim of lead and pesticide poisoning, its numbers shrinking to a mere handful by the middle of the century. Captive breeding has boosted the population to more than 120. Attempts to release condors back into the wild have run into problems—some of the birds drank antifreeze, others were electrocuted on power lines—but there are now twenty-three California condors free-flying in Northern Arizona near two release sites, the Vermillion Cliffs and the Hurricane Cliffs, both in Grand Canyon country. They seem to be thriving in their new habitat, which was likely occupied by condors a hundred years or so ago.

The whooping crane is another spectacular bird facing extinction. Decimated by hunting and the conversion of marshlands to agriculture, its numbers dropped to a handful before action was taken. The population stands at 140 birds that summer in Canada and winter in the southern U. S.

The piping plover, an East Coast seabird, is a more encouraging case. Heavy coastal development and other disturbances to the plover's beach nesting grounds caused many populations to crash, but in recent years the restriction of human activity on and near the nesting areas has produced some remarkable recoveries.

These examples underscore the possibility for improvement as well as the need for involvement. Local bird groups, animal welfare organizations, and state agencies provide a wealth of resources for the conservation-minded birder. In ways that range from tending injured and orphaned birds to reporting cruelty and poaching, volunteers are making vital contributions to the survival and recovery of bird populations, helping to ensure that bird-watching doesn't become an exercise of witnessing species vanish.

The whooping crane, an endangered bird, numbered as few as fifteen in the 1940s. Some of the cranes' eggs have been successfully raised by sandhill cranes, but those adults have failed to breed successfully among their own species.

IDENTIFICATION GUIDE

The pleasures of birding are found both in learning more about the common birds we see all around us and in identifying that elusive species we may see only once in a lifetime.

So, you're familiar with many of the characteristics that can help you identify a bird, from the way it flies down to the color of its eye ring *(pages 108-113)*. Now it's time to affix an actual name to the bird you've seen.

While there are more than nine hundred species in North America—more than most birders will see in a lifetime—some species are more common and accessible than others and represent the lion's share of viewing opportunities. These are the 150 species presented in this Identification Guide—from bluebirds to buntings, from puffins to plovers. As you become a more experienced birder, you will probably want an exhaustive field guide that will include every bird you might possibly see in your area.

The species in the guide are organized in sections according to the silhouettes described on pages 106 and 107. Within each section, the birds are ordered alphabetically by the common name of the species.

To use the guide, first identify the silhouette of the bird you've seen, then turn to the appropriate section of the guide. Study the illustrations to pick out the birds that most closely match yours. (Where plumage varies by sex and season, we've shown the distinctive male breeding plumage.) Then, narrow your possibilities by noting the habitat icon corresponding to the habitats described on pages 114 and 115—birds that are seen in many different habitats are so-marked.

To confirm your identification, note the information given on the size of the bird—as measured from the tip of the bill to the tip of its tail—its song, and its most noticeable visible characteristics, such as proportions and fieldmark-

*"No bird,
but an invisible thing,
A voice, a mystery."*

— WILLIAM WORDSWORTH
To the Cuckoo

Identifying silhouette of bird (see below)

Range of bird:
■ Summer
■ Winter
■ Year-round

Habitat where bird is most commonly found (see below)

AMERICAN AVOCET | *Recurvirostra americana*

Size: 16 to 20 inches.

Characteristics: White and black body on tall, pale-blue legs. Cinnamon or gray head and neck with long, upcurved bill.

Voice: Loud, repetitive "kleet."

Nest: Shallow depression in mudflat or sandbar; sparsely lined except in rising waters when built up with grasses and sticks.

Eggs: Four, olive with dark blotches, 2 inches.

American avocets live along lakes and mudflats, where their highly sensitive, upcurved bills and long legs are specially designed for feeding. Wading through shallow water, they sway their immersed bills rhythmically from side to side to sweep up small crustaceans and aquatic insects. When confronted by predators, avocet hatchlings can use their wings and partially webbed toes to dive twenty feet out of sight.

Fieldmarkings that help you identify the bird

Brief character sketch of bird

BIRD SILHOUETTES

▪ **SEABIRDS**

▪ **LONG-LEGGED WADING BIRDS**

▪ **GULLS AND TERNS**

▪ **SMALL WADERS**

▪ **DUCK-SHAPED BIRDS**

▪ **HAWK-SHAPED BIRDS**

▪ **OWL-SHAPED BIRDS**

▪ **PIGEON-SHAPED BIRDS**

▪ **SWALLOW-SHAPED BIRDS**

▪ **CHICKEN-SHAPED BIRDS**

▪ **CLIMBING BIRDS**

▪ **PERCHING BIRDS**

BIRD HABITATS

▪ **FORESTS**

▪ **WOODLANDS**

▪ **GRASSLANDS**

▪ **DESERTS**

▪ **INLAND CLIFFS**

▪ **SEASHORES**

▪ **LAKES AND RIVERS**

▪ **WETLANDS**

ings. If you are lucky enough to be able to take a look at the bird's nest up close, its location and construction, as well as the number and appearance of the eggs, can be additional clues.

Along with the information required to identify a species, each entry includes some interesting details about the bird, ranging from its feeding habits to its ritualistic courtship behavior.

DOUBLE-CRESTED CORMORANT | *Phalacrocorax auritus*

Size: 32 to 33 inches.

Wingspan: 52 inches.

Characteristics: Black with snakelike neck and rounded orange throat pouch. Two tufted crests, white or dark, rarely seen on crown.

Voice: Deep croaks and grunts sounded at nest.

Nest: Platform of drift material on coastal ground or in tree.

Eggs: Three or four, pale blue, nest-stained, 2.4 inches.

The double-crested cormorant is marvelously adapted for fishing. Its plumage is designed to become rapidly waterlogged, helping the bird to dive and swim deep underwater. Here it searches out schooling fish. Prey is brought to the surface and swallowed whole, the flexible neck of the cormorant adjusting to pass a larger catch. Indigestible items are later coughed up in a pellet. When not fishing, the double-crested cormorant is comfortable soaring high in the air or perched on land, upright with its wings outstretched to dry.

NORTHERN GANNET | *Morus bassanus*

Size: 37 inches.

Wingspan: 72 inches.

Characteristics: Adult, white with yellowish head, long, black-tipped wings, and pointed bill and tail. Immature, dark with white patches.

Voice: In colony, loud, rough "keruk-keruk."

Nest: Shallow platform of seaweed, dirt, and feathers, cemented with droppings.

Eggs: One, pale blue-white, nest-stained, 3.1 inches.

From heights of more than a hundred feet, the northern gannet plunges headlong into the sea to retrieve herring and other small schooling fish. The length of the dive and large size of the bird make for considerable impact at the water's surface, and the northern gannet's skull is specially reinforced to cope. In summer, the birds crowd onto northern sea cliffs, where they walk through the colony with their wings up and bills skyward to avoid provoking aggression.

PIGEON GUILLEMOT | *Cepphus columba*

Size: 13.5 inches.

Characteristics: Breeding adult, black with red legs, feet, and mouth lining; wing patch white with small black wedge. Nonbreeding, white neck and underside and mottled back.

Voice: Weak "tsik" and "peeeeo" calls.

Nest: Burrow or rock cavity lined with debris.

Eggs: One or two, pale blue-green to cream with dark marks, 2.4 inches.

The pigeon guillemot is an auk—a bird with wings well suited to diving underwater. The hardy bird lives along rocky coastlines, nimbly foraging the seabed for small fish. Only in the breeding season, in its striking breeding plumage, must it come ashore, where it is clumsy and slow. To protect against mammalian predators, it nests well out of reach and sight on rocky islands and cliffs.

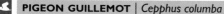

BROWN PELICAN | *Pelecanus occidentalis*

Size: 48 inches.

Wingspan: 84 inches.

Characteristics: Gray-brown with dark bill and throat pouch. Adult, white or yellow head and neck; chestnut hind neck when breeding. Immature, brown head.

Voice: Quiet "check-check" at nest. Otherwise silent.

Nest: Mound of soil and debris in scrape or saucer-like construction of sticks in mangrove tree.

Eggs: Three, white, nest-stained, 3.0 inches.

In single file, brown pelicans pass low over the coastal salt water, alternately flapping and gliding. They are extremely gregarious birds. In flocks, they dive from the air, head first, after anchovies and other fish, scooping up great bill-fuls of water and prey before surfacing. They first tilt their bills down to drain the salt water, then up to swallow the catch. They migrate together, roost together, and in the breeding season sit together on their nests, their feet cradling and warming their eggs.

ATLANTIC PUFFIN | *Fratercula arctica*

Size: 13 inches.

Characteristics: Breeding adult, black with white face and underside; hefty, grooved, colorful bill; orange legs. Juvenile and nonbreeding, dusky face and smaller, paler bill.

Voice: Brief, strident "urrr."

Nest: Burrow under rocks or excavated into soil with sparsely lined chamber.

Eggs: One, off-white with subtle markings, 2.5 inches.

The bill of the Atlantic puffin, extending from forehead to chin, looks like a clown's mask. The bill actually takes five years to develop to its full size; horny coverings, called plates, at the base of the bill are shed after each breeding season. Despite its cumbersome look, the bill is a phenomenal feeding tool. Underwater the bird will catch a small fish, place it crosswise in the bill, and catch another without releasing the first.

AMERICAN BITTERN | *Botaurus lentiginosus*

Size: 28 to 34 inches.

Characteristics: Brown with streaked underside and black outer wings visible in flight. Long neck, short legs and tail. Stocky.

Voice: Deep "pump-er-lunk" breeding call by male. "Kok-kok-kok" alarm call.

Nest: Platform of reeds and bulrushes hidden within dense marsh grasses.

Eggs: Two to seven, yellow-brown, 1.9 inches.

The American bittern is a secretive, solitary bird. It inhabits marshes and wetlands borders where its brown-streaked plumage is well hidden amongst the tall reeds and grasses. In the presence of danger, it completes its camouflage by pointing its bill upward and freezing, or better yet, swaying like the surrounding vegetation. Unfortunately, loss of wetlands has significantly reduced the population of this species.

KILLDEER | *Charadrius vociferus*

Size: 10.5 inches.

Characteristics: Brown with white underside and reddish rump. White collar with two black neck rings.

Voice: "Kill-deer, kill-deer" call.

Nest: Depression lined with pebbles.

Eggs: Three or four, yellow-brown with dark blotches, 1.4 inches.

The killdeer darts across fields, stopping as suddenly as it started to inspect the ground for insects and grubs. It is a highly adaptive plover, nesting on athletics fields, lawns, and rooftops—any natural or man-made surface with little vegetation. At its nest, the killdeer is famous for its dramatic "broken wing" display: Dragging its wing along the ground as if injured, it distracts predators away from its eggs or young.

RED KNOT | *Calidris canutus*

Size: 11 inches.

Characteristics: Chunky with short, dark legs. Breeding adult, mottled gray and brown with reddish face and breast. Nonbreeding, gray with white belly.

Voice: Low, strident "knut" feeding call. Gentle "kuret" flight call.

Nest: Shallow depression lined with lichen and leaves.

Eggs: Four, light olive-green with brown spotting, 1.4 inches.

Red knots breed in the Arctic, where their nests were first discovered during Admiral Peary's pioneering trip to the North Pole in 1909. When fall comes, the red knots return to coastal beaches and mudflats worldwide, performing impressive feats of long-distance flight. Some red knots fly clear across the Greenland ice cap to Europe, while others fly hundreds of miles over open water to South America.

BLACK-BELLIED PLOVER | *Pluvialis squatarola*

Size: 12 inches.

Characteristics: Breeding adult, speckled black and white with solid black face, neck, and underside, white undertail, black "armpits" in flight.

Voice: Long, sorrowful whistles of three notes—second in lower pitch.

Nest: Scrape lined with pebbles, grass, and moss on raised ground.

Eggs: Four, pale gray-green with dark spots, 2.0 inches.

Whether on southern beaches in winter or on Arctic tundra in summer, the black-bellied plover is highly territorial. It migrates and roosts in flocks, but needs private space to forage and nest. The male is highly involved in the nesting process. Not only does he share incubation duties, but after the female deserts the hatchlings, he stays as a single parent. Winter feeding territories are aggressively defended by individuals who scratch and probe their muddy terrain for marine animals, such as mollusks and crustaceans.

SEMIPALMATED PLOVER | *Charadrius semipalmatus*

Size: 7.25 inches.

Characteristics: Dark brown with white face, neck and underside, dark neck ring and bar extending from eye to bill; orange legs. Bill, orange with dark tip (dark overall in winter).

Voice: "Chee-wee" whistle, rising in pitch.

Nest: Shallow depression, sparsely lined, on gravel or sand surface.

Eggs: Four, brown-olive with dark blotches, 1.3 inches.

On its Arctic breeding grounds, the semipalmated plover nests, not on the tundra where many shorebirds gather, but on the riverside gravel and sandbars. The striking dark and light pattern of its plumage makes it unusually inconspicuous against this surface. The semipalmated plover forages by running, stopping, inspecting the ground, and starting off again. It hunts alone; the footsteps of a flock would probably frighten its prey—crustaceans, mollusks, and worms—into hiding.

CLAPPER RAIL | *Rallus longirostris*

Size: 14.5 inches.

Characteristics: Back feathers dark, gray-edged. Flanks dark, white-striped. Breast plumage varies from cinnamon to gray. Short tail, long legs and bill.

Voice: Series of dry notes such as "chit" that accelerates and slows.

Nest: Raised platform of grass and reeds, often with ramp and woven canopy.

Eggs: Seven to eleven, olive-yellow with dark blotches, 1.7 inches.

The clapper rail is a large rail of coastal salt marshes, not to be confused with the similar king rail, which inhabits freshwater marshes in an overlapping region. Like most rails, the clapper is highly secretive, heard more often than seen. Its call sounds mostly at dusk and dawn, ten or more notes that speed up and slow down. When the clapper does venture into the open to forage for crabs, fish, or insects, its short tail twitches and flashes white underneath.

SORA RAIL | *Porzana carolina*

Size: 9 inches.

Characteristics: Breeding adult, dark brown back with threads of white; gray, barred belly; black face and neck bordered with gray. Black is less conspicuous in winter.

Voice: Lamenting, rising "pu-wee, pu-wee" and descending whinny.

Nest: Saucer of marsh vegetation, often with ramp and canopy, a little above water.

Eggs: Ten to twelve, rich yellow-brown with brown spotting, 1.2 inches.

The sora, like other rails, has an incredible ability to compress its body widthwise. It literally thins itself to slip unnoticed through its reedy environment. The bird breeds mostly in fresh water, its nest elevated in the cattails to avoid flooding. Eggs hatch at different times, and one parent will brood while the other continues to incubate. In late summer, soras gather in large numbers to fatten up on aquatic insects and weed seeds before migrating back to southern salt marshes.

SANDERLING | *Calidris alba*

Size: 8 inches.

Characteristics: Rusty in summer, pale gray in winter; white belly, undertail, and wing stripe; long black legs and bill.

Voice: Soft "kip" flight call, often repeated.

Nest: Slight scrape lined with leaves near water.

Eggs: Four, green-olive to light brown with sparse blotches, 1.4 inches.

Up and down the sandy beaches runs the sanderling, chasing the tide. It follows the receding surf to forage for exposed sandcrabs, then beats a hasty retreat as the waves return. Its comical to-ing and fro-ing can be seen in the winter on coasts worldwide. In spring, the little sandpiper heads north to Arctic tundra. Here monogamous couples may share incubation duty at one nest or may produce two nests, one for each parent to tend.

SEMIPALMATED SANDPIPER | *Calidris pusilla*

Size: 6.25 inches.

Characteristics: Grayish brown with white underside, black legs, and straight round-tipped bill. In summer, prominent streaking above and on breast.

Voice: Brief, low "cherk" in flight.

Nest: Slight depression lined with soft plant matter.

Eggs: Four, yellowish with dark blotches, 1.2 inches.

Each spring, semipalmated sandpipers leave South America for the low Arctic tundra. The birds stop to refuel at Delaware Bay, along with crowds of other shorebirds on similar treks. At its Arctic breeding ground, the male displays over his territory, hovering and singing in a motorboat-like splutter. He nests and raises his brood, his mate departing before the young are fledged. "Semipalmated" refers to the bird's toes, which are partially webbed.

SPOTTED SANDPIPER | *Actitis macularia*

Size: 8 inches.

Characteristics: Grayish with white underside and wing stripe. In summer, dark spots on underside, dark barring above, and orange bill with dark tip.

Voice: Courtship "peetweet-peetweet." Alarm or aggression series of "weet" notes.

Nest: Slight depression lined with grass and moss concealed under vegetation.

Eggs: Four, yellow-brown with brown blotches, 1.3 inches.

The spotted sandpiper is one of the rare and impressive examples of a serial polyandrous bird. Every breeding season, the female mates with two to five males. In a way, she is no different than a polygynous male, defending a territory and competing through the summer for the increasingly scarce available mates. What makes her impressive is that to each clutch she contributes not microscopic sperm, but four eggs, equaling 80 percent of her body weight.

UPLAND SANDPIPER | *Bartramia longicauda*

Size: 12 inches.

Characteristics: Mottled brown with small head, large dark eyes, and long neck and tail. Short yellow bill, yellow legs, and white belly.

Voice: "Pulip-pulip" in flight. Breathy whistle on breeding ground.

Nest: Slight scrape with dry grass lining. Concealed under arching grasses.

Eggs: Four, pale yellow-brown with red-brown marks, 1.8 inches.

A rebel among shorebirds, the upland sandpiper—formerly the upland plover—is not found on the usual mudflats and beaches. Instead, it prefers to stand chin-deep in grasses or perched on a stump, surveying its upland field. In the breeding season, the male displays in flight with fluttering wings and a whistled song. After landing, he holds his wings above his back, a trademark of this bird in all seasons.

WESTERN SANDPIPER | *Calidris mauri*

Size: 6.5 inches.

Characteristics: Grayish brown with white underside, black legs, and straight, pointy bill. In summer, prominent streaking above, on breast, and on flank; rusty wash on shoulders, crown, and ear patch.

Voice: High, harsh "dzheet."

Nest: Slight depression, sparsely lined with plant matter, often under shrub.

Eggs: Four, yellowish brown with darker brown spots, 1.2 inches.

A close relative of the semi-palmated sandpiper, the western sandpiper is difficult to tell apart—especially on their common wintering grounds. Both species occupy open shorelines along the American coasts and by inland lakes and marshes. The western probes mud in shallow water, while the semi-palmated inspects mud at the water's edge. Virtually the entire American population of western sandpipers stops every year at the Copper River Delta in the Yukon as the birds migrate between wintering grounds and Alaska's tundra slopes.

COMMON SNIPE | *Gallinago gallinago*

Size: 19 inches.

Characteristics: Mottled brown with prominent black and white stripes on head and back. White belly. Short legs and long, straight bill.

Voice: Harsh "skipe" when flushed. Perched on breeding ground, "wheet-wheet" song.

Nest: Scrape padded with moss, grass, and leaves concealed in bog or tundra.

Eggs: Four, brown to yellow-olive, blotched with dark brown, 1.5 inches.

Sliding its long, flexible bill deep into mud, the common snipe feels for crane-fly larvae and other buried insects. With its spiked tongue and serrated bill, it lifts the prey to its throat and swallows. Much of the year, the solitary bird lives hidden in a wet grass habitat. When flushed, it virtually explodes out of the vegetation in zigzag flight. During the breeding season, it dives above its nest site, producing a whinnying noise with its vibrating outer tail feathers.

AMERICAN WOODCOCK | *Scolopax minor*

Size: 11 inches.

Characteristics: Plump with short legs and neck, and long, straight bill. Mottled brown with warm-brown underside. Big dark eyes set far back on head.

Voice: Nasal "peeent."

Nest: Scrape with leaf lining and rim of twigs on open ground with heavy leaf litter.

Eggs: Four, yellowish brown with brown markings, 1.5 inches.

Every night the American woodcock ventures out of the forest to the open fields where it plunges its long bill deep into the moist ground to feed. The bill's sensitive, flexible tip is a useful tool for grabbing earthworms. The bird's large eyes are set far back on its head giving it well-developed binocular-like vision that enables it to see to the sides and back—an advantage when the woodcock's bill is deep in the ground and predators are about.

AMERICAN AVOCET | *Recurvirostra americana*

Size: 16 to 20 inches.

Characteristics: White and black body on tall, pale-blue legs. Cinnamon or gray head and neck with long, upcurved bill.

Voice: Loud, repetitive "kleet."

Nest: Shallow depression in mudflat or sandbar; sparsely lined except in rising waters when built up with grasses and sticks.

Eggs: Four, olive with dark blotches, 2 inches.

American avocets live along lakes and mudflats, where their highly sensitive, upcurved bills and long legs are specially designed for feeding. Wading through shallow water, they sway their immersed bills rhythmically from side to side to sweep up small crustaceans and aquatic insects. When confronted by predators, avocet hatchlings can use their wings and partially webbed toes to dive twenty feet out of sight.

SANDHILL CRANE | *Grus canadensis*

Size: 41 to 45 inches.

Wingspan: 73 inches.

Characteristics: Rust feathers interspersed in gray plumage. Whitish head with red forehead patch and slender black bill.

Voice: Loud, low-pitched "karooo-karooo-karooo."

Nest: Mound of marsh plants on ground or floating in shallow water.

Eggs: Two, pale olive with dark blotches, 3.8 inches.

Every spring, a quarter of a million sandhill cranes gather by the Platte River in Nebraska, following the traditional migratory route taught to each generation by the elders of their flock. Upon arrival at their nesting grounds in northern Canada and far eastern Siberia, the sandhill cranes begin their spectacular courtship dance. Pairs bow, then leap gracefully into the air, wings outstretched, or run wings extended, calling to their mate and tossing grass into the air.

CATTLE EGRET | *Bubulcus ibis*

Size: 20 inches.

Characteristics: Short and pure white with orange bill and legs. Yellow-brown plumes on crown, back, and breast during breeding season.

Voice: "Rick-rack" call in colonies.

Nest: Shallow bowl of sticks and twigs in shrub or tree.

Eggs: Three or four, pale blue, 1.9 inches.

The cattle egret is not a native of America. It is believed to have emigrated from Africa. Unlike native herons and egrets, the cattle egret forages on land. It flocks at the feet or on the backs of horses and cattle—hence its name—catching insects that are flushed out of the grazing field. The cattle egret will fly directly into the smoke of field fires to feast on prey trying to escape the blaze.

GREAT BLUE HERON | *Ardea herodias*

Size: 46 inches.

Wingspan: 72 inches.

Characteristics: Adult, slate blue with white head and breast; black stripe over each eye extending into plume, also down foreneck; long legs and bill. Immature, black crown, no plumes.

Voice: Throaty "frahnk" and brief "rok-rok."

Nest: Flat platform of interlaced sticks lined with finer material in treetops.

Eggs: Three to seven, pale blue-green, 2.5 inches.

The largest North American heron, the great blue is also the most widespread, its habitat needs being common (calm waters) and its diet (aquatic and terrestrial animals) allowing it to winter farther north than most herons. It nests in colonies in treetops unless the ground is predator-free. The male claims and defends the territory with a lot of neck-extending, raising of breeding plumage, and bill-snapping. Both parents tend the nest—father by day, mother at night.

GREEN HERON | *Butorides virescens*

Size: 19 inches.

Wingspan: 36 inches.

Characteristics: Dark green-gray with chestnut neck and face, dark green crest, and orange-yellow legs. Compact build, short legs and neck. Long bill.

Voice: "Kyow" flight and alarm call.

Nest: Platform of interlaced sticks concealed in tree or shrub near water.

Eggs: Three to six, light blue-green, 1.5 inches.

The green, or green-backed, heron is a solitary, rather secretive bird. It inhabits a variety of watery habitats that provide dense vegetation in which to take cover and nest. It occasionally wades into open shallow waters to hunt, though it appears nervous there, raising and lowering its crest and flicking its tail. It feeds in the shallows on the fish, frogs, insects, and reptiles that pass within reach of its bill.

BLACK-CROWNED NIGHT HERON | *Nycticorax nycticorax*

Size: 25 inches.

Characteristics: Stocky with short yellow legs. Adult, gray with black back and crown, white face, and hindneck plumes. Immature, brown-streaked and spotted white.

Voice: Low, harsh "quok."

Nest: Platform of sticks, sparsely lined, concealed in reeds, thicket, or tree.

Eggs: Three to five, light blue-green, 2.0 inches.

By day, black-crowned night herons roost silent and motionless in waterside trees, keeping out of the way of aggressive day herons and egrets. Then at dusk, they lift into the air with great "quok" calls and fly to shallow foraging waters to fish. Only in the breeding season do they deviate from their nocturnal lifestyle, hunting also by day. The black-crowned night heron nests in colonies, occasionally sharing the site with other herons and ibises.

GREATER YELLOWLEGS | *Tringa melanoleuca*

Size: 14 inches.

Characteristics: Dark with white speckles, pale underside, long bill, and long yellow-orange legs. In summer, head and neck more heavily streaked; belly and flanks are barred.

Voice: Downslurred "whew-whew-whew."

Nest: Slight depression, minimally lined, concealed in moss, generally near water.

Eggs: Four, yellowish brown with dark marks, 1.9 inches.

The greater yellowlegs is one of the more vocal shorebirds. Its alarm call may alert a beach full of birds to the presence of an intruder. It summers in subarctic bogs and migrates in small but very noisy flocks to winter on coastal marshes, beaches, and mudflats. It feeds by sweeping its bill tip through shallow water and dashing after minnows and insects. In winter, it defends a feeding territory.

BUFFLEHEAD | *Bucephala albeola*

Size: 12 to 14 inches.

Characteristics: Male, white with black back, prominent white patch on back of dark green- and purple-tinted head. Female, gray-brown with white cheek stripe.

Voice: Male, squeaky whistle; female, hoarse quack. Generally silent.

Nest: Woodpecker's tree cavity lined with down.

Eggs: Six to twelve, ivory-yellow, 1.8 inches.

The oddly shaped head of this diving duck has earned it the name "buffalo head" (bufflehead for short). In wooded lakes and ponds, it streamlines its plumage, leaps slightly forward, then plunges underwater to feed on small aquatic animals and plants. It is most unusual for a diver, as it springs into flight directly from the water with no footwork, flying with quiet, rapid wing beats close to the surface. Socially it is also different from most other ducks, keeping one long-term mate and rarely flocking in large numbers.

CANVASBACK | *Aythya valisineria*

Size: 20 to 24 inches.

Characteristics: Male, white with chestnut head and neck, black breast and tail. Female, gray and brown. Distinct sloped profile and forehead; long, dark bill.

Voice: Male, croak, peep, growl, and courting "coo." Female, "quack" and soft "krr-krr."

Nest: In shallow wetlands, dense basket of dead vegetation lined with down.

Eggs: Seven to twelve, grayish olive, 2.4 inches.

The canvasback is the fastest duck in flight. It flocks in V-formation, or lines, and can reach up to seventy-two miles per hour. The canvasback is a diver, foraging on the bottom of shallow waters for its food. In the shallowest areas, it may use its feet to stir up the bottom before upending to feed. The canvasback's Latin name refers to its favorite food, *valisin eria*—wild celery.

AMERICAN COOT | *Fulica americana*

Size: 15.5 inches.

Characteristics: Slate gray plumage, small red forehead shield, and white bill with dark ring around tip. Large feet with lobed toes.

Voice: Toy-trumpetlike toots and cackles.

Nest: Floating platform of reeds lined with finer material.

Eggs: Eight to twelve, yellow-brown with dark blotches, 1.9 inches.

The American coot is not a graceful water bird. In marshy lakes and park ponds, it has earned the name "splatterer," scrambling across the water's surface, wings flapping frantically. Its splashy display is not only necessary for takeoff, but is also a way of defending territory against interlopers. The aggressive resident rushes the trespasser, then rears up and attacks with its powerful lobed feet.

AMERICAN BLACK DUCK | *Anas rubripes*

Size: 23 inches.

Characteristics: Dark brown with paler head and neck, violet wing patch, and greenish bill. Bright, silvery underwing visible in flight.

Voice: Male, "kwek-kwek." Female, "quack."

Nest: Depression in ground, padded with grass and leaves, lined with down.

Eggs: Six to twelve, off-white to green, 2.4 inches.

The black duck is the woodland's version of the mallard. The two dabbling ducks are in fact closely related and their behavior is similar. Their different habitat needs had, until recently, kept them apart.

Unfortunately, the black duck—which is actually not black but dark brown—is losing its wetlands and consequently its identity. The abundant mallard is invading what was traditionally black duck territory and overwhelming the black duck by breeding with it.

WOOD DUCK | *Aix sponsa*

Size: 17 to 20 inches.

Characteristics: Male, green-blue back and wings, green crest, red eyes and bill, brown underside; prominent white borders between colors. Female, gray-brown with white eye ring and belly.

Voice: Male, high "jeeeee" whistle. Female, louder "oo-eek, oo-eek" call.

Nest: Tree cavity lined with down.

Eggs: Ten to fifteen, off-white, 2.0 inches.

The wood duck has an interesting start to life. The first task of a hatchling is to scale the inside of its tree-cavity nest, then fling itself some thirty to sixty-five feet to the water or the ground below. Hunted for its meat, eggs, and the male's exquisitely colored feathers, the wood duck was pushed almost to extinction in the early twentieth century, before protective laws and a nest-box program helped restore its numbers.

COMMON EIDER | *Somateria mollissima*

Size: 25 inches.

Characteristics: Distinctive "Roman-nose" shape to forehead and bill. Male, white with black wings, belly, and crown. Female, brown with dark stripes.

Voice: Male, cooing sounds. Female, hoarse repeated calls.

Nest: Shallow depression in ground, padded with weeds and sticks, lined with down.

Eggs: Three to five, olive-green, 2.7 inches.

The common eider is a hardy duck that breeds in the coastal waters of the Arctic. It sometimes floats by the thousands close to shore, diving for blue mussels and other mollusks. In the breeding season, the female remains ashore to tend her eggs and may eat nothing for a month. Female common eiders are famous for the excellent insulating quality of their down. In fact, "eiderdown" has become synonymous with "feather-filled quilt."

COMMON GOLDENEYE | *Bucephala clangula*

Size: 18 inches.

Characteristics: Male, dark green head and dark back. White cheek patch, underside, and flank. Female, gray with brown head, white collar, and yellow-tipped bill.

Voice: Male, courting "eeent."

Nest: Large tree cavity near water, lined with down.

Eggs: Seven to ten, pale green to olive, 2.4 inches.

The common goldeneye is a diving bird that is also called "whistler" for the sound its rapid wing beats make in flight. The goldeneye breeds near woods that provide tree cavities for nesting. When a female cannot find a cavity, she may lay her eggs in the nest of another goldeneye. As it turns out, the host female is likely to be her sister or daughter, since female goldeneyes often return to breed at their birthplace.

CANADA GOOSE | *Branta canadensis*

Size: 25 to 45 inches.

Characteristics: Brown-gray with black head and neck, prominent white chin-strap. White rump, black tail, and white undertail.

Voice: Rich "honk-a-lonk." Smaller birds, high-pitched cackle.

Nest: Depression holding bowl of plant material, lined with down, on knoll at water's edge.

Eggs: Four to seven, white, nest-stained, 2.9 to 3.6 inches.

Each year, spring and autumn are announced by the honking fanfare of migrating Canada geese. The flocks are easily recognized for their famous V-formation. Some Canada geese have given up migration for the semi-domesticated life, residing year-round in city parks and golf courses, where they occasionally become quite bold. The range of the birds has increased in recent years, expanding rapidly into the southeast.

SNOW GOOSE | *Chen caerulescens*

Size: 28 to 29 inches.

Characteristics: Snow-white with pink bill and feet and black wingtips. Dark form (the "blue goose"), blue-gray wings and lower neck.

Voice: High-pitched "honk."

Nest: Slight depression near water's edge, lined with grass and down.

Eggs: Three to five, white, nest-stained, 3.2 inches.

Since the start of this century, the population of snow geese has climbed from near extinction to numbers in the millions. Females often return to the colony where they were born to breed. The reproductive organs of the Arctic-breeding birds shrink once eggs are laid, making it impossible for the female to produce a second clutch if the first is lost.

PIED-BILLED GREBE | *Podilymbus podiceps*

Size: 12 to 13.5 inches.

Characteristics: Brown with black throat and chin, pale belly and undertail. White bill with black ring. In winter, throat and chin white, bill ring not visible.

Voice: "Cow-cow-cow-cow-cow" call in breeding season. Alarm "keck-keck."

Nest: Platform of rotting plants anchored to stands in shallow water.

Eggs: Four to seven, pale blue-green, nest-stained, 1.7 inches.

The pied-billed grebe leads a solitary life in marshy ponds. It avoids company by hiding in vegetation or sinking chin-deep in water. It dives for insects, fish, and other small vertebrates, consuming them along with a huge number of feathers. The feathers are thought to pad the stomach, protecting it against sharp bones. Hatchling grebes often ride on their parents' backs. During foraging expeditions, they hang on with their bills as their parents dive underwater.

COMMON LOON | *Gavia immer*

Size: 32 inches.

Characteristics: Breeding adult, black hood, red eyes, black and white striped neck ring, and checkered back. Nonbreeding, gray with white throat and incomplete neck ring.

Voice: Yodel-like laugh, hoot calls.

Nest: Platform of local vegetation next to water.

Eggs: Two, greenish brown with dark spots, 3.5 inches.

With its maniacal laugh and its haunting call, the common loon is a symbol of wilderness. The bird is a graceful swimmer and talented diver with a streamlined body that plunges deep and fast after fish. It may float breast-deep or sink up to its chin, and in danger can stay underwater for up to three minutes. The skeleton of the loon includes many solid bones that provide extra weight. Its muscular legs and large webbed feet help power it forward.

MALLARD | *Anas platyrhnchos*

Size: 24 inches.

Characteristics: Breeding male, gray; bright green head and neck, yellow bill, chestnut breast, white collar. Female, mottled brown; orange and black bill.

Voice: Male, "raeb-raeb" aggressive call; brief courtship whistle. Female, "quegegege" inciting call; "quack" if uneasy.

Nest: Flat bowl of plant matter on ground near water.

Eggs: Seven to ten, light green, 2.3 inches.

In early spring, mallard pairs arrive at their breeding ground at the tail end of an intricate series of courtship rituals. Males splash water off their bills at preferred mates and also engage in tail-shaking. Meanwhile, females attempt to beguile their suitors with flirtatious, over-the-shoulder flicks of the bill. Despite this involved ceremony, the males take off together shortly after incubation begins, leaving their mates to hatch and rear the young.

COMMON MERGANSER | *Mergus merganser*

Size: 25 inches.

Characteristics: Male, white with dark back and dark green head. Female, gray with chestnut, crested head, white chin and breast. Both, thin red bill.

Voice: Male, courting guitarlike note. Female, raspy call.

Nest: Platform of plant material, lined with down, concealed in cavity, crevice, or hole.

Eggs: Eight to eleven, pale yellow-brown, 2.6 inches.

The name merganser comes from the Latin, meaning "diving goose." This is indeed a superb diver that swims effortlessly underwater, mostly in pursuit of fish. Its bill is serrated to grip its slippery prey. In early spring, small flocks migrate to wooded lakes and rivers, where they nest near water in the hidden places provided in tree cavities.

NORTHERN PINTAIL | *Anas acuta*

Size: 20 to 26 inches.

Characteristics: Male, dark with white on underside and foreneck extending in two thin lines onto rich brown head. Long, slender neck. Pinlike central tail in nuptial plumage.

Voice: Male, whistle. Female, "quack."

Nest: Slight depression, lined with vegetation and down, on dry ground.

Eggs: Six to ten, light olive, 2.2 inches.

The elegant head and neck of the northern pintail spends part of the time in the not-so-elegant underwater mud, pulling up shoots and roots. This duck is a summer resident of marshes, ponds, and lakes. It forages over wide areas and sometimes nests away from the water in sites more exposed than other ducks would dare. Northern pintails pair on the wintering grain fields and during spring migration.

NORTHERN SHOVELER | *Anas clypeata*

Size: 19 inches.

Characteristics: Shovel-shaped bill. Male, glossy green head, white breast, and auburn flank. Female, brown, darkly streaked; gray bill edged with orange.

Voice: Male, low pitch courtship "took-a." Female, "quack" and five-note call in decrescendo.

Nest: Slight depression, padded with grasses and lined with down.

Eggs: Nine to twelve, pale greenish brown, 2.0 inches.

This duck's bill—longer than its owner's head and broadest at its tip—inspired the bird's name. The bill evolved to suit the northern shoveler's filter-feeding technique: swept side to side in muddy shallows, the bill strains small aquatic animals and plant matter with its comblike edges. In spring, the bird flies to northern breeding grounds. Here the males encircle a female, and each male in turn swims or flies a short distance, hoping the female will follow him and mate.

GREEN-WINGED TEAL | *Anas crecca*

Size: 14 inches.

Characteristics: Male, gray with chestnut head and iridescent green ear patch; white vertical stripe near shoulder. Female, dark, mottled brown with white undertail and green wing patch.

Voice: Male, shrill-whistled "krick'et." Female, quacking call of four high notes.

Nest: Depression in brush or weeds, padding of twigs and grasses, down-lined.

Eggs: Six to eleven, cream to pale yellow-brown, 1.8 inches.

In early spring, green-winged teals flock north to their breeding grounds. Fast and agile in flight, twisting and turning together, they are the smallest of the North American surface-feeding, or dabbling, ducks. They breed near shallow fresh water, filtering the mud and picking the surface for plants, seeds, and insects. At summer's end, they may move hundreds of miles away to molt. They migrate south in small flocks, stopping by the thousands at common resting points.

CALIFORNIA GULL | *Larus californicus*

Size: 21 inches.

Characteristics: Adult, white with gray back and wings, black wingtips. Dark eyes, yellow bill with black and red spots near tip.

Voice: Gentle "kow-kow-kow."

Nest: Slight depression padded with plant material, feathers, and garbage.

Eggs: Two or three, brown, olive, or gray with dark marks, 2.7 inches.

The life of the California gull does not appear particularly glamorous. In winter, the bird scavenges for food in garbage dumps, seacoasts, and fields. Summer is spent inland, in tightly packed, shadeless colonies. Almost everything is eaten—from insects and fish to carrion and even the eggs and young of other birds. Nevertheless, the gull has its own monument in Salt Lake City, where it saved the Mormons from a terrible plague of grasshoppers in 1848.

HERRING GULL | *Larus argentatus*

Size: 25 inches.

Characteristics: Adult, white with pale gray mantle, black wingtips with white spot; yellow bill tipped with red spot; pink legs. Immature, mottled brown.

Voice: Long "ow-ow-ow-kee-kee-kee-kyaw-kyaw-kyaw" and choking calls.

Nest: Scrape in ground near wind barrier, lined with plant matter.

Eggs: Three, olive-brown with dark blotches, 2.9 inches.

It is hard to imagine that the herring gull was ever rare along the Atlantic coast. But before its population grew to become the urban nuisance and airport hazard that it is today, the bird was hunted to rarity for its white feathers. The law has since permitted the herring gull to keep its feathers, which serve to reflect sunlight and thus keep the bird cool. They can also transfer information: Other birds flock to feed when they notice the light-backed gulls hovering over schooling fish.

LAUGHING GULL | *Larus atricilla*

Size: 17 inches.

Characteristics: Adult, white with dark gray wings and black wingtips. When breeding, black hood and dark red bill. Immature, gray-brown.

Voice: High-pitched "ha-ha-ha-ha."

Nest: Slight depression or woven cup with fine grass lining in tall vegetation.

Eggs: Three or four, olive-brown with dark blotches, 2.1 inches.

This gull is readily identified by the high-pitched "laughing" call for which it is named. It also stands out as the only gull to breed in the heat of the southeast. Adult gulls, like other nonperching birds, can rid their bodies of excess heat through their unfeathered legs and the floor of their mouths. Gull hatchlings, however, lack these thermoregulatory abilities. Nests are built in tall vegetation, possibly to shield hatchlings from the heat and predators.

RING-BILLED GULL | *Larus delawarensis*

Size: 17 inches.

Characteristics: Adult, white with pale gray mantle; black wingtips with two white spots; yellow bill with black ring near tip. Immature, mottled brown.

Voice: "Hyah-hyah" call.

Nest: Depression or shaped as cup, lined with plant material, feathers, and debris, near water.

Eggs: Two to four, grayish olive with brown marks, 2.3 inches.

The ring-billed gull was once called the common American gull. Its numbers dropped drastically in the late nineteenth century due to the feather trade, but the bird has since regained its original status as the most common gull of inland North America. The success of the ring-billed gull can be attributed to its amazing flexibility. It can live almost any place with water and food, and food includes everything from fish and rodents to insects and worms in farm fields.

ARCTIC TERN | *Sterna paradisaea*

Size: 16 inches.

Characteristics: Adult, gray with pale underside, black cap and nape, and red bill. Very long, forked white tail.

Voice: Raspy "keer-yeer."

Nest: Scrape, occasionally lined with grass, on gravel beach or coastal tundra.

Eggs: Three, yellow-brown to olive with dark brown marks, 1.6 inches.

As its name suggests, this tern breeds in the Arctic. It nests in colonies on coasts, islands, or inland shores, reuniting each summer with its long-term mate. Some Arctic terns winter at the very opposite pole, in the Antarctic Sea, completing a 22,000-mile odyssey each year.

COMMON TERN | *Sterna hirundo*

Size: 15 inches.

Characteristics: Adult, gray with pale underside, black cap and nape, and black-tipped red bill. Long, forked white tail. Juvenile, similar with brown wash and white forehead.

Voice: Low, harsh "keear" and short "kip."

Nest: Scrape lined with grass on island or beach with low vegetation.

Eggs: Three, yellow-brown to olive with dark brown marks, 1.6 inches.

Cruising over coastal or inland waters, a breeding male scans for food. A small fish grabs his attention and he plunges headfirst into the water. He then displays his catch, parading above his breeding colony, which may number in the thousands. The females are fed through courtship until the eggs are laid, a ritual that likely demonstrates the fishing prowess of the mate and strengthens the pair bond.

BALD EAGLE | *Haliaeetus leucocephalus*

Size: 30 to 37 inches.

Wingspan: 70 to 90 inches.

Characteristics: Adult, dark brown with long, broad wings, white head, white squared tail, and yellow hooked bill. Immature, brown mottled with white.

Voice: Piercing "kark kark."

Nest: Vast platform of sticks lined with finer material in tall tree or on cliff.

Eggs: Two, blue-white, often nest-stained, 3.0 inches.

Far from being bald, this eagle has a rich crown of white plumage that likely inspired its name ("balde" in Old English means white). The bird often feasts on carrion, especially dead or dying salmon, or steals fish from smaller birds. It is also an able hunter, diving from high perches or cruising low over its watery habitat. In mating season, the bald eagle engages in spectacular aerial acrobatics with its mate, which includes locking talons and tumbling together.

GOLDEN EAGLE | *Aquila chrysaetos*

Size: 30 to 40 inches.

Wingspan: 80 to 88 inches.

Characteristics: Adult, dark brown with long, broad wings, golden nape, and feathered legs; dark, hooked bill. Immature, brown; white patch under wing and tail.

Voice: Rapid "kya-kya" on approaching nest with food.

Nest: Vast platform of sticks and roots lined with finer material in tall tree or on cliff.

Eggs: One to three, off-white with dark markings, 2.9 inches.

The territory of the golden eagle is open country where jackrabbits and other prey are easily spotted and seized. A territory will generally contain several nests belonging to the same pair and used alternately. Like the bald eagle, the golden eagle builds huge nests—some up to ten feet in diameter. The golden eagle is believed by many Native American tribes to carry mystical powers that can be obtained in a single feather.

PEREGRINE FALCON | *Falco peregrinus*

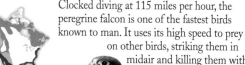

Size: 16 to 20 inches.

Wingspan: 36 to 44 inches.

Characteristics: Blue-gray streamlined body with tapered wings and long, squared tail. Black crown, nape, and moustache. White underside with dark stripes.

Voice: High-pitched, rasping "kack-kack-kack-kack."

Nest: Scrape on cliff.

Eggs: Three or four, cream with dark specks, 2.1 inches.

Clocked diving at 115 miles per hour, the peregrine falcon is one of the fastest birds known to man. It uses its high speed to prey on other birds, striking them in midair and killing them with its feet. Excessive use of pesticides almost killed off the falcons by thinning their eggshells, but captive breeding and release programs have successfully reestablished the population in the wild and in cities, where they often nest on skyscrapers.

NORTHERN HARRIER | *Circus cyaneus*

Size: 17 to 23 inches.

Wingspan: 38 to 48 inches.

Characteristics: Owl-like facial disk, long slender wings and tail, and white rump. Male, pale gray with white underside. Female, brown with streaked underside.

Voice: Shrill "kee-kee-kee-kee" or whistle at nest. Otherwise silent.

Nest: Platform of plants or lined depression on ground.

Eggs: Four to six, pale blue, nest stained, occasionally spotted, 1.8 inches.

Once known as the marsh hawk, the northern harrier hunts over marshes and open grasslands, gliding low then swooping down on rodents, small birds, and other animals. Like the owl, it has a curved facial ruff that collects sound. By flying close to the ground, the harrier can use hearing, in addition to sight, to locate prey. The aerial acrobatics of the bird are reserved for courtship, with the bird diving and looping through the air to impress potential mates.

RED-TAILED HAWK | *Buteo jamaicensis*

Size: 22 inches.

Wingspan: 50 inches.

Characteristics: Stocky with broad, rounded wings and fanned tail. Reddish tail in adult, pale chest, and dark band across belly. Rest of plumage variable.

Voice: Aggressive, downslurred "tseeeaarr."

Nest: Bulky platform of sticks with finer lining in tall tree or on cliff.

Eggs: Two or three, white with brown marks, 2.4 inches.

The red-tailed hawk is the most widespread of the North American hawks, occupying habitats with open ground for hunting and woodlands for nesting. It hunts mainly rodents, spotting them from high perches or while soaring over fields, then diving on them. The male's hunting skills are important because for a period of four to five weeks he provides all the meat to the female for feeding to the young. Once the young learn to tear up food for themselves, prey is air-dropped to them by both parents.

SHARP-SHINNED HAWK | *Accipiter striatus*

Size: 10 to 14 inches.

Wingspan: 20 to 28 inches.

Characteristics: Blue-gray with reddish brown barring on cream underside. Small head, short, rounded wings, and long, square tail.

Voice: Rapidly repeated "kek" alarm call.

Nest: Platform of sticks concealed low in fir tree.

Eggs: Four or five, pale blue with brown wash and marks, 1.5 inches.

The sharp-shinned hawk preys on small songbirds, following them in summer to the northern woodlands and in winter down to the subtropics. The wings of the sharp-shinned hawk are noticeably short—and for good reason. Hunting within dense woodlands requires maneuverability that long wings cannot provide. From hidden perches, the hawk takes off noiselessly, dives to gain speed, and glides between trees to seize its unsuspecting prey.

AMERICAN KESTREL | *Falco sparverius*

Size: 10.5 inches.

Wingspan: 23 inches.

Characteristics: Reddish brown, cream underside, and cheeks with double black sideburns. Thin, pointed wings, blue-gray on male. Long tail, black-tipped on male, barred on female.

Voice: Staccato "klee-klee-klee" if disturbed at nest.

Nest: Cavity in dead tree, giant cactus, or cliff.

Eggs: Four or five, pink with brown blotches, 1.4 inches.

The smallest North American falcon, the kestrel is a familiar sight on telephone poles and cables. It inhabits open country and occasionally cities, preying on large insects, small reptiles, mammals, and birds. The kestrel is a fast-flying raptor. Hovering in the air, the bird locates its prey, then plunges to earth, occasionally pursuing them in flight.

OSPREY | *Pandion haliaetus*

Size: 22 to 25 inches.

Characteristics: Adult, dark with white underside and head, conspicuous dark eye stripe. Dark-streaked chest patch on female.

Voice: Descending chirp in minor alarm. Rising squeal in flight display.

Nest: Bulky platform of sticks with grass and moss lining near water, in tree, or on poles.

Eggs: Three, pink-white with brown marks, 2.4 inches.

Ospreys are a common sight as they soar over the water, wings slightly crooked, then plunge to earth, snatching fish from just below the surface with their spiny, gripping toes. Sometimes, however, they misjudge their prey: There are cases of ospreys grabbing onto large fish and being forced under the water and drowned by their heavyweight targets. Even if they succeed at snaring their fish, ospreys occasionally lose their food to thieving bald eagles.

TURKEY VULTURE | *Cathartes aura*

Size: 26 inches.

Wingspan: 69 inches.

Characteristics: Dark with featherless red head. In flight, wings in shallow V with silver flight feathers; tail extends beyond feet.

Voice: Grunts and hisses while on nest or in competition for food.

Nest: Little or no added material. Sheltered in cave, crevice of cliff, hollow tree, or thicket.

Eggs: Two, whitish with brown marks, 2.8 inches.

The turkey vulture rises at its communal roost and stretches its wings in the sun to warm itself. It takes off from the roosting tree or building and soars over the semi-open country, rocking from to side. It flaps occasionally while soaring, borne upward on thermals and updrafts that can lift the vulture higher than 10,000 feet. It scans for carrion, preferably fresh, sometimes relying on its extremely keen sense of smell.

BARN OWL | *Tyto alba*

Size: 16 to 18 inches.

Characteristics: Reddish brown with white heart-shaped facial disk, dark eyes, and white to cinnamon underside. Slim with long legs.

Voice: Raspy hissing and screeching call.

Nest: In tree cavity, cave, abandoned burrow, barn, or church steeple. No lining.

Eggs: Three to eight, white, nest-stained, 1.7 inches.

A nocturnal hunter, the barn owl often appears quite supernatural, its pale figure taking wing from its roost at sunset. In the darkness, the owl's vision is excellent, but totally dispensable. The bird's secret weapon is its hearing. Flying with silent wing beats, the barn owl can pick up a mouse footfall thirty yards away. The sound is channeled by the facial ruff to the asymmetrically positioned ears, which enable it to divine the location of its unlucky prey.

EASTERN SCREECH OWL | *Otus asio*

Size: 9 inches.

Characteristics: Small with mottled red and gray phases. Yellow eyes; ear tufts can be concealed.

Voice: Whiny on changing pitch. Single-pitch song.

Nest: Old woodpecker's hole or natural tree cavity.

Eggs: Three to five, white, 1.4 inches.

The eastern screech owl appears in two distinct color phases, gray and red, which can be found at any time of the year. The coloration serves as a camouflage, allowing the owl to blend in with branches when roosting immobile on a perch. In courtship, the male blinks his large yellow eyes at his intended and with great ceremony offers her dinner. Once mated, they preen each other and may roost and nest together in the same cavity for years.

GREAT HORNED OWL | *Bubo virginianus*

Size: 22 inches.

Characteristics: Large and dark with barred and streaked underside. Ear tufts, white throat, and rusty face.

Voice: Five or six deep hoots delivered in personalized rhythm.

Nest: Old hawk's, eagle's, crow's, or heron's nest, lined with breast feathers.

Eggs: Two or three, dull white, 2.2 inches.

The largest of the "horned" owls in North America, the great horned owl feasts on a variety of creatures as large as grouse or as small as insects, varying with the owl's habitat—desert, swamp, forest, and city. Prey are taken at night, spotted from a high perch. In the most daring hunts, the great horned owl goes after skunk and porcupine, though capturing a porcupine can often prove as fatal to the attacker as to the attacked.

SNOWY OWL | *Nyctea scandiaca*

Size: 23 to 24 inches.

Characteristics: White with black bars and spots mostly on females and juveniles. Brilliant yellow eyes set in round white face.

Voice: When breeding, barking call. Otherwise silent.

Nest: Slight depression on raised tundra; little or no lining.

Eggs: Three to eleven, white, often nest-stained, 2.2 inches.

The incubation of the snowy owl begins before the last egg is laid, so the owlets hatch at intervals. This strategy reflects the trouble the snowy owl faces with its unpredictable food supply. Lemmings are its principal summer prey, and their abundance determines where the snowy owl nests, if at all, and the clutch size. In low lemming years, asynchronous hatching may ensure that at least the eldest owlet gets a decent meal without sibling competition.

WHIP-POOR-WILL | *Caprimulgus vociferus*

Size: 10 inches.

Characteristics: Intricate pattern of grays and browns, paler on underside. Dark throat underlined by white or yellowish brown necklace. Rounded wings and tail tip.

Voice: Endless song of "whip-poor-will" phrases.

Nest: Open floor of woodlands; no added material.

Eggs: Two, white with brown and gray marks, 1.2 inches.

At rest by day on the forest floor, the whip-poor-will virtually disappears, cloaked in plumage of mottled browns and grays. When foraging in flight, the short bill tip that protrudes from the bird's face opens into a gaping, bristled mouth almost as wide as the whip-poor-will's head. Insects are simply swept in. Prey is most visible by moonlight, so the whip-poor-will times its nesting to be feeding its young under a full moon.

NORTHERN BOBWHITE | *Colinus virginianus*

Size: 9.5 to 10 inches.

Characteristics: Mottled reddish brown with short gray tail. Prominent throat patch and stripe above each eye, white on males, yellow-brown on females.

Voice: "Bob-bob-white" whistle.

Nest: Shallow depression in ground with lining and arched roof of grasses.

Eggs: Twelve to fifteen, unmarked white to cream, 1.2 inches.

The bobwhite is a native species of quail, named for its male's distinctive spring mating call. It was once a popular and plentiful game bird. Early farming practices provided it with the patchwork environment of different vegetation and cover it requires in summer, and the population flourished. With the decline in the number of shrubby fence rows separating small farms, the number of these birds has diminished. The bobwhite is a sociable bird. In fall and winter, bobwhite families assemble into coveys, or groups, of ten to thirty.

RUFFED GROUSE | Bonasa umbellus

Size: 17 inches.

Characteristics: Reddish or gray, mottled. Black neck ruff and crest. Fan-shaped, multibanded tail with large black band near tip.

Voice: Female cooing and clucking. Male, quickening drumming.

Nest: Concealed depression lined with plant material and preened feathers.

Eggs: Nine to twelve, yellowish brown, occasionally spotted, 1.5 inches.

From the floor of the northern woodlands comes the mating call of the male ruffed grouse—not a conventional song or whistle, but a "drumming" generated by rapid wing beats against the air. The ruffed grouse is a year-round resident of the woods. To cope with the cold winters, it grows long leg feathers, develops snowshoe-like feet, and roosts in the snow, sometimes burying itself beneath it.

SAGE GROUSE | Centrocercus urophasianus

Size: 28 inches.

Characteristics: Mottled gray-brown, with black belly, feathered feet, spiked tail; yellow eye comb, black throat, white ruff, and inflatable sacs on male's chest.

Voice: Male, "wa-um-poo" popping call. Female, "kuk-kuk-kuk" call.

Nest: Depression under sage bush sparsely lined with grass and sage leaves.

Eggs: Seven to nine, olive speckled evenly with brown, 2.2 inches.

The life of the sage grouse is undeniably bound to the sagebrush: It is a permanent resident of sage country; builds its nest, lined with sage leaves, under sagebrush; and in fall and winter eats almost nothing but sage leaves and shoots. The bird is best recognized for the male's extraordinary chest sacs. In spring, the males assemble at traditional sites (leks) and strut, tails fanned, rapidly inflating and deflating their sacs, generating a "popping" mating call.

RING-NECKED PHEASANT | Phasianus colchicus

Size: 21 to 33 inches.

Characteristics: Male, mottled iridescent bronze, green, and brown; metallic green hood, red wattles, and broad white neck ring. Female, mottled brown. Both, long, pointed tail.

Voice: Male, territorial "skwagock." Female, response "kia-kia."

Nest: Slight depression lined with grass and leaves, concealed by dense cover.

Eggs: Ten to twelve, olive-brown, unmarked, 1.6 inches.

A native of Asia, the ring-necked pheasant was introduced to North America in 1850 as a game bird. Brush and farmlands provide waste grains, seeds, berries, and insects for foraging, as well as dense cover for nesting. The bird roosts and may also forage in trees. In winter, the birds live in unisex flocks. By spring, however, the males regain separate territories. Each male may attract a harem of females to nest and raise his young.

ROADRUNNER | *Geococcyx californianus*

Size: 22 to 23 inches.

Characteristics: Streaked brown and white with bushy crest and long, solid bill. Long legs and tail. Blue and red stripe behind eye.

Voice: Low, descending, dovelike "coo."

Nest: Platform of sticks with fine lining in cactus, tree, or bush.

Eggs: Four to six, white with yellow tint, 1.5 inches.

Although a well-known cartoon made this bird famous, some details of its biology need correction. First, the roadrunner does not say "beep beep;" it coos. It does run quickly through desert and open country, but only up to fifteen miles per hour—perhaps in faster spurts when chasing a lizard or another bird. (Ninety percent of its diet is animal.) One cartoon trait is true: Stop a roadrunner in its tracks and up go its crest and tail.

WILD TURKEY | *Meleagris gallopavo*

Size: 36 to 49 inches.

Characteristics: Dark and iridescent with featherless pink and blue head and red wattles. Male, larger, shinier, with tuft of feathers on breast.

Voice: Male, gobbling call. Female, yelping response. Clucking notes.

Nest: Slight depression, with meager lining, concealed in vegetation.

Eggs: Ten to twelve, yellow-brown to white with brown marks, 2.5 inches.

Benjamin Franklin proposed this bird as the national emblem of the United States. It lost to the bald eagle by just one vote. The wild turkey is a slender, cautious bird that walks and runs about oak woodlands and roosts in tall trees. The male displays its full glory in spring. With feathers puffed, tail and wings spread, and the fleshy appendage on its throat (wattles) swollen, it gobbles to attract a mate.

MOURNING DOVE | *Zenaida macroura*

Size: 12 inches.

Characteristics: Gray-brown, sleek, with long, pointed tail, large black dots on upper wing. Male, lighter-colored head and iridescent neck.

Voice: Mournful "ooahoo-oo-oo-oo" call.

Nest: Loose platform of twigs in tree, shrub, or on building ledge.

Eggs: Two, unmarked white, 1.1 inches.

Perched on telephone and power lines, the mourning dove is a common sight from city parks to farmlands. The bird raises more broods each year—up to six—than any other North American bird. It nurses its young on its own "milk," which it produces in a pocket of the throat called the crop. Adult males and females regurgitate the protein- and fat-rich fluid, feeding it to their hatchlings for a few weeks as they wean them onto a diet of seeds.

BROWN CREEPER | *Certhia americana*

Size: 5.25 to 5.75 inches.

Characteristics: Brown-streaked with white underside and long, stiff, pointed tail. Thin downcurved bill. Long, sharp claws.

Voice: High-pitched song of repeated whistles. Soft "tsee" call.

Nest: Hammocklike cup of twigs, bark, and moss under loose bark or in cavity.

Eggs: Five or six, white with reddish brown speckles, 0.6 inch.

The brown creeper is a master of camouflage: With its belly pressed against a tree trunk, it is virtually invisible. Its brown-streaked plumage has evolved to resemble bark—a good thing since the brown creeper spends most of its time on tree trunks. "Creeper" refers to this bird's painstakingly slow foraging habits. Starting at the base of a tree, it crawls up the trunk in a spiral fashion, probing for insects and grubs left by less attentive feeders.

NORTHERN FLICKER | *Colaptes auratus*

Size: 12 to 14 inches.

Characteristics: Back and wings brown with black bars; underside whitish, spotted with black. Colorful undertail and wings. Whiskers on male.

Voice: Loud, repeated "wik" and single "klee-yer" call.

Nest: Cavity excavated in dead wood with no added lining.

Eggs: Five to eight, white, 1.1 inches.

This woodpecker lives in most habitats with trees and open ground. The openness is important because, unlike most woodpeckers, the northern flicker forages on the ground for ants. The bird comes in two morphs. The yellow-shafted flicker of the east and north has yellow under its tail and wings, black whiskers (male), and a red crescent on a gray nape. The red-shafted flicker in the west has red under its tail and wings and red whiskers (male).

RED-BREASTED NUTHATCH | *Sitta canadensis*

Size: 4.5 inches.

Characteristics: Gray with reddish brown underside. Black cap and eyeline frame a prominent white eyebrow. Female, gray cap and paler underside.

Voice: Quiet nasal "nyeep-nyeep" and brief "tsip" calls.

Nest: Cavity excavated in rotting wood, padded with plant matter and feathers.

Eggs: Five to seven, white, occasionally pinkish, speckled with auburn, 0.6 inch.

The adult red-breasted nuthatch doesn't linger or perch at the entrance to its nest. Smeared around the cavity hole is gluey pitch, applied by the parents in the course of nest construction, probably to protect against predators or to reduce parasites in the nest. The tree-clinging bird nests in the northern coniferous woods. In years when the conifer seed crop is good, it remains for the winter and gathers in groups in the old nesting cavities to roost.

WHITE-BREASTED NUTHATCH | *Sitta carolinensis*

Size: 6 inches.

Characteristics: Gray with black cap, white face and breast, rusty belly and rump.

Voice: Nasal "ank-ank" call.

Nest: Cup of twigs, grass, bark, and hair.

Eggs: Five to nine, white with dark spots (particularly at larger end), 0.8 inch.

Unlike brown creepers and woodpeckers that forage along bark in the expected heads-up, tails-down orientation, the gravity-defying white-breasted nuthatch takes on tree trunks upside down. From this rather original perspective, the bird can spot those tasty insects that slipped the eye of upright foragers. White-breasted nuthatch pairs occupy a year-round territory in deciduous or coniferous forests.

YELLOW-BELLIED SAPSUCKER | *Sphyrapicus varius*

Size: 8.5 inches.

Characteristics: Mottled black and white with red forehead, white face, and black eyeline. Yellowish belly and large white wing patch.

Voice: "Weep-weep" and "churr" calls.

Nest: Excavated hole in deciduous tree, lined with wood chips.

Eggs: Five or six, white, 1.0 inch.

When the "tatatat-tatat-tatat" drumming of the yellow-bellied sapsucker sounds from the woods and orchards, the male and female are performing a courtship duet. They then use their bills to drill a series of holes in a tree. Later, the birds return to feast on the sap that has oozed from the holes or on the insects attracted by the liquid.

HAIRY WOODPECKER | *Picoides villosus*

Size: 9 inches.

Characteristics: White with white-spotted black wings and black striped face. Male, bright red crown patch.

Voice: Sharp "teek" contact call. Courtship "wicki-wicki-wicki."

Nest: Cavity, lined with wood chips, excavated in live deciduous tree or dead conifer.

Eggs: Four, white, 1.0 inch.

Where there are large trees, the hairy woodpecker may be heard pecking into trunks in search of insects. In late winter when the pecking sound is rhythmic and resonant, it is the courtship drumming of the male and female. In spring, for some twenty days, a lighter, irregular tapping is produced as the pair excavates a nesting cavity. For this life of bill-pounding, the hairy woodpecker (like all woodpeckers) is fortunately well equipped with a fluid-lined skull to absorb shock.

PILEATED WOODPECKER | *Dryocopus pileatus*

Size: 18 inches.

Characteristics: Crow-sized; black with flaming red crest and white stripe up side of neck. White face with black eye band and cheek band. Male, red cheek band.

Voice: "Cuk" notes exchanged between mates. Courtship or territorial "wuck-a wuck-a wuck-a."

Nest: Cavity bored in dead wood.

Eggs: Three to five, white, 1.3 inches.

Propped against a tree trunk, the pileated woodpecker pries and pounds its way through dead wood, carving out its trademark feeding hole: a rectangle three to six inches long. With its extendable tongue, it fishes out its main prey: the tunneling carpenter ants. When the tongue is retracted, it wraps around the skull just under the bird's thick skin. It is part bone, part muscle, and is coated in sticky saliva and spiked at the tip for improved insect retrieval.

 RED-HEADED WOODPECKER | *Melanerpes erythrocephalus*

Size: 8 inches.

Characteristics: Trademark brilliant red head. Black with white underside, rump, and wing patch.

Voice: Harsh, low "kweeer."

Nest: Cavity excavated in live or dead wood.

Eggs: Four or five, white, 1.0 inch.

The red-headed woodpecker is possibly the most omnivorous of all woodpeckers. Rather than simply boring for insects, this woodpecker forages on the ground, along tree limbs, and in foliage, feasting on insects, berries, acorns and nuts, and even the occasional nestling or bird's egg. In preparation for winter in its open wooded habitat, it stores caches of food in small cavities, sealing these off with splinters of wet wood and guarding them against unwelcome starlings and blue jays.

PURPLE MARTIN | *Progne subis*

Size: 8 inches.

Characteristics: Male, dark, shiny purple with long black wings and black notched tail. Female, duller with whitish gray underside.

Voice: "Cher-cher" call near nest. Pair's song, two notes, then throaty trill.

Nest: Cup of mud and plant matter with raised edge at front. Or, in "apartment-like" birdhouse.

Eggs: Four or five, white, unmarked, 1.0 inch.

The purple martin is best known as the communal bird that lives in large houses with scores of occupants. The practice of providing houses for the birds goes back centuries, when Indians from southern tribes placed groups of hollow gourds in their gardens. Today nest competition from starlings and house sparrows is contributing to a decline in the numbers of North America's largest swallow.

COMMON NIGHTHAWK | *Chordeiles minor*

Size: 10 inches.

Characteristics: Dark with paler underside. Forked tail. Long, pointed wings with large white wing bars near tips. Male, white throat and tail bar.

Voice: Nasal "peent."

Nest: Eggs laid directly on gravel or dirt.

Eggs: Two, pale olive, darkly speckled, 1.2 inches.

An opportunistic and adaptive bird, the common nighthawk ranges far and wide, from forests and plains to towns and cities. Gravel roofs serve as well as gravel pits for nesting, and the city electric lights, swarming with winged insects, provide convenient "fly-by" meals. The courtship display of the male is spectacular. Circling and hovering above his mate and nest site, he enters a steep dive, his wings generating a hollow "twanging" as he nears the ground.

BARN SWALLOW | *Hirundo rustica*

Size: 7 inches.

Characteristics: Black and shiny blue; cinnamon underside, red-brown chin and throat. Deeply forked tail and long pointy wings.

Voice: Twittering song punctuated with occasional harsh sounds. Feeding or alarm "chit-chit" call.

Nest: Cup of mud and straw, feather-lined, often on building ledge or beam.

Eggs: Four or five, white with brown spots, 0.8 inch.

With few cliffs and caves to choose from, the barn swallow resorts to barns and bridges to build its mud cup nest. Both female and male collect mud. It may take a thousand trips and two weeks to complete the job. The couple court in aerial chases and engage in intimate bill-touching, head-rubbing, and preening. At the nest, the male aggressively guards his mate to help ensure that the eggs he incubates and the young he rears are his own.

TREE SWALLOW | *Tachycineta bicolor*

Size: 6 inches.

Characteristics: Male and adult female, iridescent blue-green with white underside extending to cheek but not eye. Immature female, gray-brown with increasing blue; white underside.

Voice: Song, three down-slurred notes, then warble. "Chee-deep" alarm call.

Nest: Cup of grass lined with feathers in tree cavity.

Eggs: Four to six, pale pink becoming white, 0.8 inch.

The nest cavity of the tree swallow is a popular place. In spring, many cavity nesters vie for the site. Later, when a tree swallow pair settles in, young females frequently visit the home. Still in immature plumage, they are not chased away, so they check out the nesting female, looking to replace her should her health fail. Finally, when the chicks hatch, juveniles join the family at their nest—not to help out, but to steal food.

RED-WINGED BLACKBIRD | *Agelaius phoeniceus*

Size: 8.5 to 9.5 inches.

Characteristics: Male, shiny black with brilliant red shoulder patch bordered in yellow. Female, brown with heavily streaked underside, pointy bill, and whitish eyebrows.

Voice: Musical "o-ka-lee" song ending in trill. Common "check" calls.

Nest: Cup woven low in stands of grass or reeds.

Eggs: Three to five, pale green-blue with dark markings, 1 inch.

Although gregarious in winter, the red-winged blackbird is ferociously territorial during the breeding season. A male will claim more than a half acre of wetlands and vigorously defend it by displaying his red-wing badges, singing, and attacking intruders, no matter their size. If a male's search for food or space leads him into another's territory, he may choose to hide his red badge and avoid arousing the anger of the resident. Some males boast up to as many as fifteen mates.

YELLOW-HEADED BLACKBIRD | *Xanthocephalus xanthocephalus*

Size: 9.5 to 10.5 inches.

Characteristics: Male, black with bright yellow head, black mask, and white wing patch. Female, gray-brown with yellow chin and breast, and white-streaked underside.

Voice: Guttural "check" and "chuck" calls. "Kuk-koh-koh-koh-waaaaaaaa" song.

Nest: Bulky weaved cup of aquatic vegetation, lashed to bulrushes or other marshy stands.

Eggs: Three to five, pale gray-green, 1 inch.

Outside the breeding season, yellow-headed blackbirds live harmoniously with red-winged blackbirds, starlings, and cowbirds in huge, mixed flocks. By the thousands, they land in fields to forage for waste grains. But in the summer, the male yellow-headed blackbird becomes a bully, forcing his red-winged relative out of the deeper, insect-rich marshlands to establish his own territory where food is most abundant.

EASTERN BLUEBIRD | *Sialia sialis*

Size: 6 to 7 inches.

Characteristics: Brilliant blue top with chestnut breast and white belly. Female, plumage color less vivid.

Voice: Soft melodic "chur-chur-lee-chur-lee" song. "Chur-lee" call.

Nest: Cup of twigs and weeds lined with finer grasses in cavity in tree.

Eggs: Four or five, pale blue or occasionally white, unmarked, 0.8 inch.

A hundred years ago, the eastern bluebird was common in the open country. Its population then suffered a dramatic fall as its cavity nesting sites were eliminated or aggressively taken over by house sparrows and starlings. Meanwhile, pesticides and herbicides contaminated and reduced its diet of berries and summer insects. In 1978 a campaign was launched to rehouse the eastern bluebird, which has helped in the recovery of this much-loved songbird.

MOUNTAIN BLUEBIRD | *Sialia currucoides*

Size: 7.5 inches.

Characteristics: Bright blue with powder blue underside. Female, plumage colors less vivid. Thinner bill and longer wings than eastern bluebird.

Voice: Low, quavering "tru-lee" song. Thin "few" call.

Nest: Loose cup of weeds and twigs in cavity of tree, sometimes cliff or building.

Eggs: Five or six, unmarked pale blue, occasionally white, 0.8 inch.

As its name suggests, the mountain bluebird breeds in the open country of foothills and mountains. It dines on summer insects, darting from its perch or hovering over fields, then dropping to seize its prey. In winter, it flocks by the hundreds to pinyon-juniper woods, open lowlands, and deserts to forage for berries. Because of the remote nature of its breeding grounds, the mountain bluebird has not suffered like its eastern relative from the competition of other cavity nesters.

BOBOLINK | *Dolichonyx oryzivorus*

Size: 6.5 to 8 inches.

Characteristics: Male, black with yellow-brown nape, white shoulders, and rump. In winter, resembles female, yellow-brown with darkly striped head and streaked back.

Voice: Bubbly "bob-o-link" song. Repeated "ink" call.

Nest: Depression in ground, padded with coarse grasses and weeds and finer lining.

Eggs: Four to seven, cinnamon with dark blotches, 0.8 inch.

The bobolink breeds mostly in hayfields since much of its preferred grassland habitat is now lost. Unfortunately, the recent practice of cutting hayfields early is threatening the species, killing many of its unfledged young. The bobolink is named after its male's summer song. It is also known as the white-winged blackbird and the ricebird for its habit of dining in rice fields as it flocks south for the winter.

INDIGO BUNTING | *Passerina cyanea*

Size: 5.5 inches.

Characteristics: Male, deep blue with blackish wings and tail. In winter, blue is obscured by brown plumage. Female, dark brown with faintly streaked, paler underside and faint wing bars.

Voice: High-pitched, paired whistles—"tsee-tsee," "tew-tew." Short "spit" call.

Nest: Woven cup of dried grass, leaves, and bark lined with finer material.

Eggs: Three or four, white or bluish white, 0.8 inch.

From his perch in the brushy pasture or wood's edge, the male indigo bunting announces his territory with hearty song. The bird is a gregarious migrator and has contributed greatly to our knowledge of avian navigation. Studies with captive indigo buntings in a planetarium revealed that the birds use the position of the stars to orient their migrations. Indigo buntings sometimes hybridize with lazuli buntings where their ranges meet.

PAINTED BUNTING | *Passerina ciris*

Size: 5.5 inches.

Characteristics: Male, brightly colored, blue head, green nape, red underside, rump, and eye ring, blackish wings and tail. Female, leaf-green, lighter underside.

Voice: Thin, musical trilling song. Short "chit" call.

Nest: Woven cup of grasses, weeds, and leaves, lined with finer material.

Eggs: Three or four, whitish blue or gray with brown spots at large end, 0.8 inch.

The origin of this bird's name is easy to fathom. The male's unusual "painted" appearance has inspired not only its common name but also the nickname *nonpareil*, meaning "incomparable." Contrary to the showy nature of his plumage, the male painted bunting seems shy, hiding within the low, dense brush of semi-open country. But to defend territory, the male sometimes engages in bloody and even fatal battles.

NORTHERN CARDINAL | *Cardinalis cardinalis*

Size: 8 to 9 inches.

Characteristics: Male, bright red with black face, crest, and conical beak. Female, yellow-brown with red wings, tail, crest, and bill.

Voice: Whistle in repeats of three—"cheer-cheer-cheer." "Chip" call.

Nest: Cup of grasses, twigs, and leaves, lined with finer material.

Eggs: Two to five, off-white to pale blue or green with dark markings, 1 inch.

The cardinal is an extremely popular songbird, the official bird of no less than seven states in the U.S. Its rich red plumage, similar to the robe of a church cardinal, earned it its name. In spring, both sexes whistle softly to attract a mate. In a tender feeding ritual, the male will approach the female and pass her a seed, touching beaks momentarily. Once a nesting territory is established, the male cardinal becomes highly aggressive and is intolerant of male cardinal trespassers.

GRAY CATBIRD | *Dumetella carolinensis*

Size: 9.5 inches.

Characteristics: Gray with black cap; long black tail, hidden chestnut undertail.

Voice: Single phrases mimicking other birds' songs. "Mew" alarm call.

Nest: Bulky cup of grass, twigs, and leaves with lining of finer material.

Eggs: Three to five, blue-green, very occasionally with red spots, 0.9 inch.

The catbird may not rival other birds in plumage, but its personality is wonderfully comical. Its call sounds like a cat (hence its common name) and rather than having a song of its own, the bird borrows from others (hence its nickname "Carolina mockingbird"). Courtship displays are most entertaining. The male chases a female, stops to sing and strut, then turns away and flashes his chestnut undertail.

BLACK-CAPPED CHICKADEE | *Parus atricapillus*

Size: 5.25 inches.

Characteristics: Short and plump with black cap and bill and white cheeks. Long gray tail and dark wings edged with white.

Voice: "Chick-a-dee-dee-dee" call.

Nest: Tree cavity lined with down, feathers, hairs, and mosses.

Eggs: Six to eight, white lightly speckled with brown, 0.6 inch.

The black-capped chickadee is best known for its acrobatics in trees, foraging at odd angles for insects, seeds, and berries, often feeding upside down. A frequent visitor to feeders, the bird will also occasionally seize sunflower seeds from an outstretched hand. During the winter, the black-capped chickadee must store as much fat as its small frame will allow. On frigid nights, it actually lowers its body temperature to conserve energy.

BROWN-HEADED COWBIRD | *Molothrus ater*

Size: 7 to 7.5 inches.

Characteristics: Male, shiny green-black with dark brown head and gray stubby bill. Female, gray-brown, lighter, faintly streaked underside.

Voice: Thin-pitched whistle. Call is "check" or rattlelike noise.

Nest: Nest of other birds.

Eggs: One per host nest, white with dark blotches, 0.8 inch.

Each breeding season, the female brown-headed cowbird may lay up to forty eggs (hence the nickname "songbird chicken") in the nest of different birds that are then expected to tend the parasite egg and resulting chick. Some birds have learned to outwit the cowbird, specifically destroying the foreign egg, rebuilding the nest over the parasitized clutch or simply abandoning the nest. Others, like the endangered Kirtland's warbler, lose many broods to the practice.

RED CROSSBILL | *Loxia curvirostra*

Size: 5.75 to 6 inches.

Characteristics: Brick-red body with forked black tail and black wings; bill with crossed tips. Female, gray with yellowish olive.

Voice: Rapid trill song. "Jip-jip-jip" flight call.

Nest: Cup of twigs, small roots, and grasses, lined with finer material.

Eggs: Three or four, whitish blue or green with dark markings mostly at large end, 0.8 inch.

With its crossed tips, the bill of the red crossbill looks impractical. But it is, in fact, a well-adapted foraging tool. Perched in a conifer, the crossbill uses its peculiar bill to pry apart the scales of cones to free the coniferous seeds on which it feeds. Since a good cone crop is unpredictable, the red crossbill spends much of the year wandering about in large flocks in search of a seed source. Once found, the flock sets up territories and nesting begins.

AMERICAN (COMMON) CROW | *Corvus brachyrhynchos*

Size: 17 to 21 inches.

Characteristics: Charcoal-black plumage, feet, and bill. Fan-shaped tail. Eyes turn from blue in juvenile to brown in adult.

Voice: "Cah-cah."

Nest: Broad, thick basket of twigs, grasses, and bark, lined with softer material.

Eggs: Four to six, bluish green with dark markings, 1.6 inches.

Common crows are among the most intelligent of birds. They have been observed dropping mollusk shells on rocks to crack open the shells. While many North American birds suffered from the increasing presence of man, the common crow quickly learned to take full advantage. Whether on farms or in urban garbage, it finds plenty of plant and animal stuff on which to feed. A crow can eat its own weight in food in a single day. The bird is also a very talented mimic.

HOUSE FINCH | *Carpodacus mexicanus*

Size: 5.5 inches.

Characteristics: Male, brown-streaked with orange-red head, bib, and rump. Short bill and squared tail. Female lacks orange-red coloring.

Voice: Musical trill ending in nasal "wheer."

Nest: Open cup of plant material, in natural or artificial cavity.

Eggs: Four or five, pale blue, speckled mostly at large end, 0.8 inch.

The house finch is a native of the southwest lowlands. It was brought east by New York City pet-store owners who sold it illegally under the name of Hollywood finch, then, threatened with prosecution, released it. The very adaptable bird has since made itself at home in cities, suburbs, and farms. It forages in flocks for weed seeds, blossoms, and berries, as well as at backyard feeders.

PURPLE FINCH | *Carpodacus purpureus*

Size: 6 inches.

Characteristics: Male, raspberry-red with brown-streaked back, white belly and undertail. Female, brown-streaked except for undertail; white cheek and white eyebrow.

Voice: Long, sweet trill. Short "pik" flight call.

Nest: Tight cup of plant material, finely lined, placed on tree branch.

Eggs: Three to six, light blue-green with some dark blotches, 0.8 inch.

The male of the species looks, as one observer described it, like a sparrow dipped in raspberry juice. When courting, the male approaches a female with his red chest puffed out, his tail cocked, and his wings low. He may carry in his bill a very unsubtle offering of nest material. As he sings to the female, he vibrates his wings, lifting himself six to twelve inches into the air. If his display is successful, the pair will nest together in the woods until fall, when small flocks assemble for migration.

GREAT CRESTED FLYCATCHER | *Myiarchus cinerascens*

Size: 8 inches.

Characteristics: Dark olive with rusty-brown tail, bright yellow belly and undertail, gray throat and breast. Bushy crest and large bill.

Voice: Loud, rising "wheep" and rolling "prreet" call.

Nest: Deep tree cavity filled with plant material, soft lining, and decorated with shed snakeskin.

Eggs: Four to six, creamy with dark markings, 0.9 inch.

The great crested flycatcher breeds in the high canopy of leafy forests, its nest concealed in natural tree cavities or woodpecker holes—the only eastern flycatcher to nest in this manner. The bird has the curious habit of decorating its nest or cavity entrance with shed snakeskin. Some birders suggest that the practice discourages would-be predators from entering the nest. Given the chance, the bird will even decorate its nest with plastic wrappers.

PACIFIC-SLOPE FLYCATCHER | *Empidonax difficilis*

Size: 5.5 inches.

Characteristics: Greenish brown with yellow underside and olive "vest." Conspicuous pale eye ring and orange lower mandible. Pale wing bars. Long tail.

Voice: Rising "suweet," repeated, occasionally interrupted with "pik."

Nest: Cup of plant matter, lined with fine material, close to ground.

Eggs: Three or four, creamy with brown marks concentrated at large end, 0.7 inch.

The Pacific-slope flycatcher of the west coast and the nearly identical Cordilleran flycatcher of the western interior were once classified together as the western flycatcher. The Pacific-slope flycatcher is distinguished by its single-syllable "suweet" (versus the double-syllable "whee-seet" of the Cordilleran) and by its coastal, slightly damper woods habitat. Both flycatchers feast on the wing, darting from shaded perches or hovering over foliage to snatch up insects.

BLUE-GRAY GNATCATCHER | *Polioptila caerulea*

Size: 4.5 inches.

Characteristics: Blue-gray with long black tail, black wingtips, and white eye ring. Underside and tail gray-white. Thin bill. Black eyebrow on breeding male.

Voice: Fretful "zeeeee" call.

Nest: Compact cup of plant material and spider webs, decorated with lichen, finely lined.

Eggs: Four or five, whitish blue spotted red-brown, 0.6 inch.

The blue-gray gnatcatcher is a lively inhabitant of the woodlands. It darts among trees and shrubs, its trademark long tail cocked or flicking about, seizing insects at its perch or in midair. In summer, the female tours a male's territory and the potential nesting sites there. One horizontal tree limb will be chosen and the pair will build a nest, camouflage it with lichen, and settle in to raise a brood or two.

AMERICAN GOLDFINCH | *Carduelis tristis*

Size: 5 inches.

Characteristics: Male, rich yellow with black cap, wings, and forked tail. White wing bars, undertail and rump. Female, green-yellow and lacks cap.

Voice: Twitters and short trills. "Perchikoree" flight call.

Nest: Compact cup of plant matter bound with spider webs and softly lined.

Eggs: Four to six, pale blue, 0.6 inch.

The American goldfinch is often called the wild canary for the male's plumage and canarylike song. A relatively late breeder, it nests in July and August among the thistles and weeds of open woods or roadsides. The female builds the nest, so tightly woven it can hold water, then lays and incubates the eggs. Meanwhile, the male climbs about the flowers and weeds, foraging for seeds to bring her. The bird is a frequent visitor to feeders, where it favors sunflower seeds.

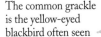 **COMMON GRACKLE** | *Quiscalus quiscula*

Size: 12 inches.

Characteristics: Male, black with dark purple-blue iridescent head, neck, and breast. Female, brown with flat, shorter tail.

Voice: Succession of harsh sounds ending in "leeek." "Chuck" call.

Nest: Thick cup of plant material and mud, lined with fine grasses and horsehair.

Eggs: Four or five, pale green-brown with dark spots, 1.2 inches.

The common grackle is the yellow-eyed blackbird often seen striding about suburban lawns and farmers' fields or nesting in local conifers, often in large flocks and always making a nuisance of itself. The grackle's notoriously bad behavior includes stealing insects and earthworms from robins and occasionally killing adult house sparrows and the eggs and nestlings of various birds. The common grackle's winter roosts may number in the millions.

EVENING GROSBEAK | *Coccothraustes vespertinus*

Size: 8 inches.

Characteristics: Male, yellow with black wings and tail and white wing patch; dark head with yellow eyebrows. Female, gray-brown with yellow nape; black and white wings and tail.

Voice: Interrupted trilling song. Ringing "peer" call.

Nest: Cup of loosely assembled twigs, lined with finer material.

Eggs: Three or four, blue to blue-green with dark blotches, 1.0 inch.

Evening grosbeaks love seeds. In winter, they wander in large flocks searching for a good supply. The introduction of box elders and bird feeders in the Northeast has helped this chunky western finch to expand its breeding range eastward. In spring, the bill of the male turns from pale yellow to lime green to signal the start of the breeding season.

ROSE-BREASTED GROSBEAK | *Pheucticus ludovicianus*

Size: 8 inches.

Characteristics: Male, black with white wing patch, belly, and rump, red breast and "armpits." Female, gray with white wing bars, eyebrows, and streaked breast; yellow "armpits."

Voice: Musical, whistled song. Squeaky "eek" call.

Nest: Loose cup of twigs, weeds, and leaves, lined with finer material.

Eggs: Three to five, light blue with dark marks, 1.0 inch.

The aptly named rose-breasted grosbeak is heard in spring and summer in woodlands, singing what sounds like a hurried variation on the American robin's whistle. A courting male will pull back his head, spread his wings and tail, dance about, and serenade a female. The female sings a shorter song to communicate with her mate. Together the pair may raise two broods, the male tending the first while the female starts on a second.

BLACK-CHINNED HUMMINGBIRD | *Archilochus alexandri*

Size: 3.5 inches.

Characteristics: Male, iridescent green with whitish underside, green flanks, deep violet throat patch, and black chin. Female, green with whitish underside. Both, needlelike bill.

Voice: High-pitched squeals and soft descending "tchew."

Nest: Deep cup of plant down and fiber, bound with cobwebs and camouflaged with lichen and dead leaves.

Eggs: Two, white, unmarked, 0.5. inch.

The black-chinned and the ruby-throated hummingbirds are closely related and similar in their calls and displays. In summer, while the ruby-throated occupies the east, the black-chinned breeds in the dry, semi-arid lowlands of the west. The males of both species have an iridescent throat patch. At the right angle, it appears brilliant violet or red; otherwise it looks black, the result of overlying transparent cells that reflect violet and red wavelengths differently depending on the intensity of the light.

RUBY-THROATED HUMMINGBIRD | *Archilochus colubris*

Size: 3.5 inches.

Characteristics: Male, iridescent green with whitish underside, green flank, and ruby-red throat patch. Female, green with whitish underside.

Voice: High-pitched squeaks in aggression.

Nest: Deep cup of plant down and fiber, bound with cobwebs and camouflaged with lichen and dead leaves.

Eggs: Two, white, unmarked, 0.5 inch.

It was the ruby-throated that earned its entire family the name hummingbird. In flight, its up to eighty wing beats per second generate audible humming. In territorial displays, the sound is intensified to intimidate the intruder. In the male's famous courtship pendulum display, it is again exaggerated: The male dives, passes the female humming louder than ever, then rises up in the air, pauses, and repeats the same U-shaped trajectory.

RUFOUS HUMMINGBIRD | *Selasphorus rufus*

Size: 3.5 inches.

Characteristics: Male, cinnamon-red with green crown and iridescent scarlet throat patch. Female, bronze-green with white underside and reddish tail and flanks, throat dotted with red and green.

Voice: Hissing "chup" and "zeee-chuppity-chup."

Nest: Cup of plant down bound with cobwebs, hidden by lichen and moss.

Eggs: Two, white, unmarked, 0.5 inch.

Because of their size, hummingbirds were never believed capable of flying great distances. Some observers claimed that they regularly rode as passengers on larger birds. Quite the contrary, the rufous hummingbird, one of the smallest hummingbirds, flies a migratory route: two thousand miles between Alaska and Central America. Despite its size, the bird is very aggressive and vigorously defends its feeding territory.

BLUE JAY | *Cyanocitta cristata*

Size: 11 to 12 inches.

Characteristics: Crested, cobalt blue with white underside. Broad black collar and finer necklace. White patches and black barring on wings and tail.

Voice: Sharp "jay-jay-jay" cry. Flowing "kloo-loo-loo" whistle. Hawk call imitation.

Nest: Solid cup of plant and manmade material, lined with fine rootlets.

Eggs: Four or five, yellow-brown, green, or blue with brown spots, 1.1 inches.

The blue jay's feathers are not, in fact, blue. They appear that color only because of the way light refracts off their inner structure. Crush a feather underfoot and the illusion is lost. The raucous bird is a master of illusions. In the spring, in eastern woodlands, it often imitates the red-shouldered hawk, sending songbirds fleeing from their nests for cover, and then feasts on the unprotected eggs and young.

GRAY JAY | *Perisoreus canadensis*

Size: 12 inches.

Characteristics: Gray with white forehead, cheek, and collar, dark cap, and pale underside. Notably fluffy and silky down. Small bill.

Voice: Whistled "yoo-yoo" in alarm. Repeated low "chuck."

Nest: Solid shallow cup of cocoons, spider silk, and bark, lined with soft material, In conifer.

Eggs: Three or four, pale green or gray with olive spots, 1.2 inches.

The gray jay is a sweet-whistling, plush-looking member of the crow family. It is called "camp robber" for its brazen way of floating into campsites and stealing food right off plates. Also known as the Canada jay, it lives year-round among the balsam firs and spruces of northern forests, nesting and raising its young in early spring when the snow is still thick on the ground.

STELLER'S JAY | *Cyanocitta stelleri*

Size: 11.5 inches.

Characteristics: Indigo with black head, crest, and upper breast. Black barring on wings and tail.

Voice: Harsh, single or repeated "shaack."

Nest: Jagged cup of plant matter, cemented with mud and lined with finer material, in conifer.

Eggs: Four or five, light blue-green with brown spots, 1.2 inches.

The Steller's jay lives in woodlands along the northwest coast and in western mountains, where coniferous trees provide it with a staple diet of acorns and pine seeds. It is a permanent resident, although in winter it occasionally flocks to lower elevations. During the breeding season, the Steller's jays form pairs. The male courts his prospective mate, feeding her seeds, the seasonal insects, bird's eggs, and small rodents and reptiles.

DARK-EYED JUNCO | *Junco hyemalis*

Size: 6 inches.

Characteristics: Plumage varies with geographical race. All have dark head and eyes, pale bill, white belly and outer tail feathers.

Voice: Single pitch warble. "Tsip," "zeet," and "kew-kew" calls.

Nest: Cup of weeds, moss, and pine needles, lined with finer material, concealed on the ground.

Eggs: Three to five, whitish blue or gray with dark blotches, 0.8 inch.

There are five races of dark-eyed junco. The two most common versions are the slate-colored and the Oregon juncos. The slate-colored version is found in the east, with dark gray males and gray-brown females. In the west: the Oregon junco with brown-back and black (male) or gray (female) hood. The birds run and hop across the leaf- and snow-covered floors of woodlands, foraging for seeds and insects, and frequently visit bird feeders.

BELTED KINGFISHER | *Ceryle alcyon*

Size: 13 inches.

Characteristics: Blue-gray with ragged crest and large bill. White collar and underside and blue breast band. Female, extra reddish band.

Voice: Low, rattling flight call.

Nest: Unlined chamber at end of tunnel excavated in dirt bank.

Eggs: Five to seven, white, 1.4 inches.

Belted kingfishers build nests in banks, with the birds taking turns at constructing, one burrowing with its oversized bill, the other behind kicking out the loosened sand. The eggs are incubated alternately by the parents. When one mate approaches the nest, it gives a personalized call to alert its partner within. The belted kingfisher always lives near clear fishing water. It hovers or perches, then dives for fish. Fledglings learn this technique by retrieving dead prey dropped by parents.

GOLDEN-CROWNED KINGLET | *Regulus satrapa*

Size: 3.5 inches.

Characteristics: Gray-olive with pale underside; white wing bars, eyebrows; black cap. Male, orange crown patch with yellow border. Female, yellow crown patch.

Voice: High-pitched "tsee-tsee-tsee" call. Accelerates into warble song.

Nest: Saclike cup of plant matter, lined with fine material, hung on conifer branch.

Eggs: Eight or nine, creamy with dark blotches, 1.5 inches.

A mite of a bird, the golden-crowned kinglet is rivaled in diminutive size by only the hummingbird. It is surprisingly hardy for such a small bird, wintering in woodlands across much of the continent, including the cold northern states and coastal provinces. The kinglet inhabits mainly coniferous woodlands, the dense foliage concealing its nest in summer and sheltering the bird from the cold in winter.

RUBY-CROWNED KINGLET | *Regulus calendula*

Size: 4.25 inches.

Characteristics: Grayish green with pale underside, two white wing bars, and white eye ring. Male, red crown patch, rarely visible.

Voice: Descending "tew" notes, then "tsee-tsee-tsee" or other three-part phrases.

Nest: Saclike cup of plant matter, lined with fine material, hung on conifer branch.

Eggs: Seven to ten, creamy with brown blotches, 0.5 inch.

The ruby-crowned kinglet is an expressive, even hyperactive bird, continuously flicking its wings and often singing from the woods and brush much more loudly than one would expect from such a small bird. It hops or hovers around branches, foraging for insects, occasionally darting to catch one in midair. Only the male of the species is crowned, displaying it in courtship and in alarm, much like the red-winged blackbird and its wing patch.

HORNED LARK | *Eremophila alpestris*

Size: 7 to 8 inches.

Characteristics: White or yellow face, throat, and belly. Black "horns," bib, and facial stripe. Dark tail with white outer feathers.

Voice: High-pitched "zeet" or "tsee-titi" call. Soft twittering song.

Nest: Grass-lined depression with pebbly "doorstep" near grass clump or manure.

Eggs: Three to five, pale greenish gray with brown marks, 0.8 inch.

In the early spring, the male horned lark performs an awesome courtship display, rising high up into the air to sing, circle, and hover, before diving toward the ground where he struts, "horns" raised, before the female. Serenading in flight appears the only option of this songbird, as the open habitat it occupies offers no perches. Larks are in fact ground dwellers, preferring to run or walk in low vegetation rather than hop among trees and brush.

BLACK-BILLED MAGPIE | *Pica pica*

Size: 19 inches.

Characteristics: Black with white flank, belly, and wing patches. Wings and long tail both iridescent green. Black bill.

Voice: High "mag" call. Repeated "chuck" notes.

Nest: Cup of mud or manure lined with plant matter, enclosed in stick dome.

Eggs: Five to eight, green-gray, speckled brown, 3.0 inches.

A talented mimic, the black-billed magpie is well known for its incessant chattering. It occasionally perches on the backs of cattle and sheep, picking off parasites. The bird experienced hard times in the 1930s when farmers and ranchers misjudged it as a pest. Contests were organized to wipe out the bird. The magpie's tendency to feed on scraps, carrion, and stolen prey did not help its situation; thousands died from ingesting poisoned baits left out for predators.

EASTERN MEADOWLARK | *Sturnella magna*

Size: 9 inches.

Characteristics: Brown with black markings, rich yellow underside, black "V" breast band, and white outer tail. Eastern, gray cheek; more prominent crown stripes.

Voice: Rattling flight call. Eastern, "dzeert" call; "seeoo-seeyeer" song. Western, "chup" call; brief, low flutelike song.

Nest: Dome of grasses hidden in dense grass stands.

Eggs: Three to seven, white, darkly speckled, 1.1 inches.

Eastern and western groups of meadowlark were only recently isolated from one another, but as they rarely hybridize, they are considered distinct species. Meadowlarks in both eastern and western meadows engage in an energetic spring courtship display. Facing the female, the male spreads his tail and flicks his wings in excitement, points his bill skyward, and fluffs his chest. The female may return the posture while the male jumps into the air.

NORTHERN MOCKINGBIRD | *Mimus polyglottos*

Size: 10 to 11 inches.

Characteristics: Gray with paler underside, white outer tail and wing patches conspicuous in flight.

Voice: Original and borrowed phrases in three or more repetitions.

Nest: Cup of vegetation on platform of twigs.

Eggs: Three to five, blue-green with brown blotches concentrated at the large end, 1.0 inch.

The mockingbird imitates a squeaky gate, a barking dog, and other noises that seem out of place in a bird's song. This is not mimicry; the bird does not wish to be taken for a gate by a trespasser or, worse still, by a potential mate. Rather, the mockingbird is practicing "vocal appropriation," drawing from local sounds to increase its song repertoire. The greater the repertoire, the more successful the male is in defending a breeding territory and attracting a mate.

CLARK'S NUTCRACKER | *Nucifraga columbiana*

Size: 12 to 13 inches.

Characteristics: Gray with black wings and white wing patch on inner trailing edge. Black inner and white outer tail feathers. Long sharp bill.

Voice: Long, raspy, and nasal "kraaaa" call.

Nest: Cup of plant matter and hair, on platform of twigs and bark, in conifer tree.

Eggs: Two to four, light green with dark marks, 1.3 inches.

Every fall, this amazing hoarder stores thousands of pine nuts all over its territory. The position of each cache is recalled in relation to a landmark. If the landmark is shifted a certain distance, the bird will search in frustration that very distance away from its cache. The hoarding behavior of the Clark's nutcracker is mutually beneficial to both bird and pine trees: The bird gets to nest and feed a family; the trees get free propagation of their seeds.

BALTIMORE ORIOLE | *Icterus galbula*

Size: 8.5 inches.

Characteristics: Male, fiery orange with black head, back, wings, and inner tail. Female, dull orange, mottled brown-black head, and dark wings.

Voice: "Hew-li" call. Song, irregular series of "hew-li" and other notes.

Nest: Saclike cup of woven plant fibers with fine lining, hung from deciduous tree branch.

Eggs: Four or five, pale blue to gray, dark blotches mostly at large end, 0.9 inch.

The Baltimore oriole was named for Lord Baltimore, whose coat of arms bore the bird's striking orange and black colors. At one time, this bird was grouped with the more western Bullock's oriole under the name northern oriole, but it has since regained its distinct species status. In summer, the Baltimore oriole occupies open woodlands and suburban shade trees. In winter it migrates, females and juveniles in flocks, males solitary, to the tropics.

OVENBIRD | *Seiurus aurocapillus*

Size: 6 inches.

Characteristics: Olive-brown with white underside. Dark dashed lines lengthwise along chest and flank. Orange crown between two dark stripes. Conspicuous white eye ring.

Voice: Crescendo of "teacher-teacher-teacher." Sharp "chip" call.

Nest: Dome of plant material on ground with single slit for entrance.

Eggs: Four or five, white with dark blotches, 0.8 inch.

This is a bird more often heard than seen, its "teacher, teacher, teacher" call growing louder as it sings out from the undergrowth. The ovenbird's name derives from its ovenlike-shaped nest. The bird is a summer resident of woodlands with closed canopy and sparse groundcover. It walks about leaf litter, poking for insects and worms. In fall, it migrates by night to the thickets and forests of the Caribbean, Mexico, and Central America.

EASTERN WOOD-PEWEE | *Contopus virens*

Size: 6 inches.

Characteristics: Dark gray-olive with pale throat and wing bars, white or yellow belly, and gray chest. Peaked crown. Bill, black with orange below.

Voice: High plaintive whistle "peeahwee-peeoh" with long pauses except in dawn song.

Nest: Snug cup of plant matter and cobwebs, camouflaged with lichen.

Eggs: Three, creamy to white, dark blotches mostly near large end, 0.7 inch.

The eastern and western wood-pewee are identical but for their range and song. They occupy the open woods of North America in summer, each species on its half of the continent. The males sing throughout the breeding season, in the east "peeahwee," in the west "fee-rrr-reet," mostly at dawn and dusk when the phrases are delivered in rapid sequence and at great lengths. The females are chased through the treetops in courtship. Each will build her nest and incubate, her mate foraging in flight for insects to feed her.

EASTERN PHOEBE | *Sayornis phoebe*

Size: 7 inches.

Characteristics: Brownish gray with black bill. White underside with olive flanks and breast. Belly yellow in autumn.

Voice: Raspy "fee-be." "Chirp" call.

Nest: Cup of moss and grass built up from mud base on waterside ledge.

Eggs: Four or five, white, 0.8 inch.

This flycatcher is unmistakable, with its namesake song and gentle tail pumping when perched. Like other flycatchers, it forages on the wing, often just over water where insects hatch and swarm. The advance of humans into the eastern phoebe's range has actually helped the bird. Previously its population had been restricted by a limited number of good stream-side nesting sites. Today it may choose from bridges, building ledges, and a large number of other man-made structures.

AMERICAN PIPIT | *Anthus rubescens*

Size: 6.5 inches.

Characteristics: Grayish brown with underside and eyebrows rich yellow-brown in fall, whitish in winter. Breast streaking most conspicuous in winter.

Voice: Rapidly repeated "chiwee" song. Sharp "peet-peet" flight call.

Nest: Cup of coarse grasses and weeds, finely lined, on sheltered ground.

Eggs: Four to six, grayish white, heavily speckled, 0.8 inch.

On Arctic tundra and mountaintops, the male American pipit advertises for a mate. Rising fifty to two hundred feet in the air, the male spreads his wings, turns his tail up, and plummets to the ground, singing all the while. Although territorial during this breeding season, the American pipit is otherwise gregarious. It migrates in large flocks to flat, open wintering grounds, feasting on the grass and weed seeds of plowed fields and the worms and crustaceans of shores and shallow waters.

COMMON RAVEN | *Corvus corax*

Size: 24 inches.

Characteristics: Crowlike with larger bill, throat feathers, and wedge-shaped tail.

Voice: Low-pitched, extended "gronk."

Nest: Basket of branches and twigs, lined with softer material, on cliff, in tree, or on building.

Eggs: Four to six, greenish with brown blotches, 2.0 inches.

This is the largest of the perching songbirds, intelligent and adaptable. A talented hunter, it works in pairs to flush out prey. It eats fruits, seeds, eggs, chicks, insects, rodents, even shellfish, which it cracks open by air-dropping onto rocks. The raven lives in a great range of habitats, from hot deserts to the freezing Arctic, thick forests to mountains. Breeding couples perform a courtship display of aerial acrobatics, bill-touching, and mutual preening.

COMMON REDPOLL | *Carduelis flammea*

Size: 5.5 inches.

Characteristics: Pale with brown-streaked flanks and rump, black chin, and red cap. Male, rosy red on breast, also on cheeks in summer.

Voice: "Chit-chit" and rising "sweeyeet" calls. Warbles and buzzes in song.

Nest: Cup of plant matter lined with ptarmigan feathers and other soft material.

Eggs: Four or five, light green to blue with dark blotches concentrated at large end, 0.7 inch.

The throat pouch of the common redpoll is its key to survival. The tiny finch lives in the north, breeding in the tundra shrub, then flocking to brushy areas only slightly to the south. In this cold climate, it must stay sheltered and waste little energy while still getting plenty of food. Knocking the seeds from trees and shrubs to the ground, the redpoll picks them up and stores them in a pocket midway down the neck for a later feast.

AMERICAN REDSTART | *Setophaga ruticilla*

Size: 5.25 inches.

Characteristics: Male, shiny black with white belly and undertail; orange patches on wings, tail, and sides. Female, gray-olive, white underside, yellow patches.

Voice: Variable sequence of high-pitched notes with final downslurred note.

Nest: Cup of grasses, decorated with lichen and bark, feather-lined, in shrub or small tree.

Eggs: Four, off-white with brown blotches, 0.6 inch.

The American redstart is a true exhibitionist. It always keeps its tail fanned and wings spread, whether perched or in flight, to show off its colorful patches. The bird is a warbler, although it acts more like a flycatcher, darting from perch to perch. Like a flycatcher, it also has large bristles by its mouth for sensing flying insects. Both parents share in the raising of their brood of four chicks.

AMERICAN ROBIN | *Turdus migratorius*

Size: 10 inches.

Characteristics: Dark gray with reddish orange underside and white undertail. White crescent above and below eye. Yellow bill. Female, paler than male.

Voice: Flowing "cheeryup-cheerily" whistle. "Tseeep" flight call and fast "tuk-tuk-tuk" call.

Nest: Mud-based cup of twigs and grasses, fine-lined, on branch or ledge.

Eggs: Four, pale blue, generally unmarked, 1.1 inches.

As hard as it might be to imagine, the American robin—the songbird that heralds the arrival of spring in many parts of North America—was at one time popularly eaten. Today the robin is a common sight hopping across a suburban lawn, halting briefly to cock its head so the most sensitive part of its vision, located in the central area of its eye, can detect earthworms in the grass.

PINE SISKIN | *Carduelis pinus*

Size: 5 inches.

Characteristics: Brown, streaked all over. Paler underside and yellow on wings and at base of tail. Slender pointy bill.

Voice: Warble song. "Sweeyeet" and rising "zrreeeee" calls.

Nest: Cup of plant material lined with feathers, hair, and moss concealed in conifer.

Eggs: Three or four, light greenish blue with dark blotches concentrated at large end, 0.7 inch.

Highly gregarious, these sparrowlike birds live in coniferous and mixed woods in summer, feasting on seeds, insects, buds, and nectar. They feed by working their way systematically down the branches and then flying up in a circular motion to start at the next tree. In fall and winter, they may flock with the goldfinch, a thousand or so birds roaming through semi-open country, occasionally flying southward.

CHIPPING SPARROW | *Spizella passerina*

Size: 5.5 inches.

Characteristics: Brown-streaked with pale gray underside, face, and nape, chestnut crown, black eye-line, and whitish eyebrow (summer). In winter, eyebrow yellowish and head brown-streaked.

Voice: Single pitch, continuous trill.

Nest: Cup of plant matter lined with fine grass and hair.

Eggs: Three or four, blue-green, dark marks mostly at large end, 0.7 inch.

Since the start of the twentieth century, life has not been the same for the chipping sparrow. The gregarious songbird was once the American urban sparrow. A native of open coniferous woods, it had adapted to breeding in town gardens and parks, eating insects and foraging for seeds. The absence of very tall trees, from which the bird likes to sing, may account for its urban decline. This sparrow once was popularly known as "hairbird" because it used abundantly available horsehair to line its nest, but the nickname was dropped as mechanized transport largely replaced horses.

HOUSE SPARROW | *Passer domesticus*

Size: 6 inches.

Characteristics: Male, gray-brown with dark-streaked back; chestnut eye-to-nape stripe; black bib. Female, brown-streaked, gray underside, and yellow eyebrows.

Voice: "Chirup-chireep-chirup" song. "Chilup" call.

Nest: Cavity padded with plant matter and garbage, lined with feathers and hair.

Eggs: Three to six, white to pale blue or green with dark spots concentrated near large end, 0.9 inch.

In 1851 a few pairs of house sparrows were introduced in Brooklyn to help control weevils. It took only fifty years for the bird to overrun the entire country, aggressively ousting bluebirds and swallows from their cavity nests. When the Model T was introduced, grain feed and grain-spread horse manure became rarer, and—as with the chipping sparrow—the house sparrow population began its decline. It is still found throughout most of North America, however, and never very far from human habitation.

SONG SPARROW | *Melospiza melodia*

Size: 6 inches.

Characteristics: Brown with pale underside; streaked back, flank, dotted breast. Gray crown stripe, eyebrows. Long rounded tail.

Voice: Song of three or four notes, buzzy "tow-wee," and warble. "Tsip" and "tchump" calls.

Nest: Cup of grasses, bark and leaves, lined with finer material.

Eggs: Three to five, green-to blue-white with reddish brown spots, 0.8 inch.

There are some thirty subspecies of song sparrows living in various habitats throughout North America. It is not unusual to spot the sweet-singing bird flying between shrubs, pumping its tail. Not that the bird tries to be visible. Quite the contrary; it leads a solitary, secretive life. In spring, song sparrows fill the shrubby fields, wood edges, and lawns, each male singing to advertise his half- to one-and-a-half-acre territory.

WHITE-THROATED SPARROW | *Zonotrichia albicollis*

Size: 6.5 inches.

Characteristics: Red-brown with gray underside, white throat. Crown and eyebrows white or tan, between dark crown and eye stripes.

Voice: Whistle, two single, three triple notes—"pure-sweet-Canada-Canada-Canada." "Tseeet" in flocks.

Nest: Cup of grasses, twigs and pine needles, fine-lined, concealed under shrub.

Eggs: Four or five, blue-green with red-brown marks, 0.8 inch.

There are two forms, or morphs, of white-throated sparrows, a white-streaked (WS) and a tan-streaked (TS), based on crown and eyebrow color. In summer, when they breed in the clearings in northern woods, an interesting pattern emerges: No pair holds two mates of the same morph. The WS male, singing in defense of his nesting territory, is more aggressive toward other singing birds than the TS male. The WS female trills in courtship and is consequently chased away by the WS male, which mates instead with the silent TS female.

EUROPEAN STARLING | *Sturnus vulgaris*

Size: 8 inches.

Characteristics: Stocky with short, squared tail. In summer, glossy black; yellow bill. In winter, white and bronze speckles; black bill.

Voice: Stream of original and imitated squeaks, trills, chips, and twitters. Brief "chjjj" in flight.

Nest: Cavity in tree padded with twigs, grasses, flowers, garbage, and feathers.

Eggs: Four to six, pale blue with brown spots, 1.2 inches.

The European starling was introduced to the U.S. in 1890 for an obscure reason: It was mentioned in one Shakespearean work and therefore, according to the American Acclimatization Society, should be imported. The bird has since overrun North America, endangering native cavity nesters and generally earning the reputation of "pest." During its summer molt the bird grows feathers with white tips. By the time spring rolls around, the white spots have faded away.

SCARLET TANAGER | *Piranga olivacea*

Size: 7 inches.

Characteristics: Male, scarlet with jet-black wings and tail; in winter, yellowish green replaces red. Female, olive with yellowish underside and gray-brown wings.

Voice: Male, series of raspy two-syllable whistles "zureet-zeeyeer-zeeroo." Female, "chip-burr" call.

Nest: Cup of grasses, twigs, and rootlets, fine-lined.

Eggs: Four, light blue-green with brown marks concentrated at large end, 0.9 inch.

The brilliant red coat of the male scarlet tanager is designed to catch the eye of a potential mate—not that of a bird-watcher. In deciduous trees where the scarlet tanager breeds, a birder may find the male surprisingly hard to spot as he flits about in the leafy upper canopy, singing and fly-catching. For a female, he is more cooperative and will perch on a branch below her, drooping his wings to display his vibrant color.

WESTERN TANAGER | *Piranga ludoviciana*

Size: 7 inches.

Characteristics: Male, yellow with red face (yellow in winter) and black back, tail, and wings. Female, olive with brown wings and gray back; some with gray chest and belly.

Voice: Song, series of gentle two- or three-syllable phrases. "Pit-er-ic" call.

Nest: Cup of moss, twigs, and rootlets with finer lining on conifer branch.

Eggs: Three to five, pale bluish green with brown marks, 0.9 inch.

The western tanager migrates north from tropical pine-oak woods, passing through grasslands and even deserts before reaching its breeding grounds in the western alpine forests. Here the male sings from late spring through the summer to defend his territory. He courts a female, chasing her through the pine and spruce; they mate and nest. Both parents forage to feed the young, fly-catching and inspecting foliage and flowers for insects, berries, and nectar.

BROWN THRASHER | *Toxostoma rufum*

Size: 11 inches.

Characteristics: Red-brown with heavily streaked, paler underside. Long tail and downward-curved bill.

Voice: Song of improvised, twice-repeated phrases. Occasionally appropriates calls of other birds. Call, loud crackling "smack."

Nest: Stick-based cup of plant matter with fine lining.

Eggs: Four or five, bluish white, finely speckled with reddish brown, 1.0 inch.

The name "thrasher" may seem apt, as this bird sweeps its bill through leaf litter and soil in search of insects. The similarity between name and foraging technique, however, is actually a coincidence—"thrasher" was originally "thrusher." The bird lives in thickets and shrubs. In fall and winter, it may rise into trees to forage for acorns and berries. In spring, the male belts out the largest known repertoire of songs of any North American bird.

HERMIT THRUSH | *Catharus guttatus*

Size: 7.5 inches.

Characteristics: Brown with reddish tail and darkly spotted, pale underside. Fine white eye ring.

Voice: Song, flutelike whistles, the first note long, followed by several notes at higher pitch.

Nest: Bulky cup of grasses, decayed wood, and moss with soft lining.

Eggs: Four, light blue or bluish green, occasionally with black flecks, 0.8 inch.

Early this century, the hermit thrush occupied the moist eastern woodlands, but gradually competition from the wood thrush pushed it onto drier terrain. Today, from west coast to east coast, the hermit thrush occupies a wide range of habitats, from sphagnum bogs to dry pine-oak woods. It is a shy bird, but may be seen perched, slowly lifting and lowering its tail, crying "chuck."

WOOD THRUSH | *Hylocichla mustelina*

Size: 8 inches.

Characteristics: Olive-brown with reddish wash. Dark-streaked white face with fine, white eye ring. Dark-spotted white underside.

Voice: Song of repeated notes followed by higher-pitched flutelike notes.

Nest: Bulky cup of plant matter and mud, lined with soft materials.

Eggs: Three or four, pale blue-green, unmarked, 1.0 inch.

The wood thrush is the boldest of the thrushes. It migrates by night from tropical forests to damp deciduous woodlands of the east, where the male aggressively defends nesting territory against the other thrushes. The personality of the wood thrush has not protected it from its greatest enemy, the cowbird. Wood thrush nests are commonly parasitized, turning out more cowbirds than they do thrushes, severely affecting the population.

TUFTED TITMOUSE | *Parus bicolor*

Size: 5 inches.

Characteristics: Small, gray, and crested with black forehead, pale breast and belly, and rusty flanks.

Voice: Downslurred, whistled "peter-peter-peter" song.

Nest: Cavity padded with plant matter, lined with animal hair.

Eggs: Five to seven, white, brown-speckled, 0.7 inch.

The tufted titmouse can often be seen hanging upside down in deciduous woodlands. Titmouse pairs winter together in small flocks, then, before spring, regain their separate territories. The males gather at territory borders to fire their songs at one another. The females prepare the nests, lining the insides with feathers, sometimes plucked right from the source—their own bodies.

EASTERN TOWHEE | *Piplio erythrophthalmus*

Size: 8 inches.

Characteristics: Black male, brown female, with chestnut flanks and white belly. White wing patch and tail patch. In west, wings and back spotted with white.

Voice: "Drink-your-tea" with end drawn out. "Chewink" and "tow-whee" calls.

Nest: Cup of plant material lined with fine grass.

Eggs: Three or four, creamy to light gray with brown spots mostly at large end, 1.0 inch.

Like the Pacific-slope flycatcher, the eastern towhee is a bird only recently added to North American checklists. What was once considered regional variation in the voice and appearance of the rufous-sided towhee is now evidence of two towhee species: the eastern towhee and the spotted towhee in the west. Both birds are often found in brushy undergrowth, scratching at leaf litter for insects and seeds and bathing in the dew that drips from vegetation.

RED-EYED VIREO | *Vireo olivaceus*

Size: 6 inches.

Characteristics: Dark olive with white underside. Blue-gray cap. White eyebrow bordered by black eyeline below and second black eyebrow above. Red eye.

Voice: Whistled song of brief, monotonous phrases. "Nyaah" and "tjjj" calls.

Nest: Basketlike cup of plant material suspended by its rim from forked twig.

Eggs: Four, white with dark blotches near large end, 0.8 inch.

Not only is this vireo red-eyed, it is also very nearsighted. It forages up close to foliage and flowers, examining them for insects or, in winter, for tropical berries. It occasionally loses some of its winter fare to the yellow-margined flycatcher with which it flocks. But the farsighted flycatcher more than repays the favor by spotting danger in the distance.

BLACK-THROATED GREEN WARBLER | *Dendroica virens*

Size: 5 inches.

Characteristics: Male, olive-green; yellow face, olive eyeline, ear patch; black throat, breast; white, black-streaked underside; yellow undertail. Female, duller; streaked throat and breast.

Voice: Song, accented "zee-zee-zee-zoo-zee," unaccented "zoo-zee-zoo-zoo-zee."

Nest: Deep cup of bark, moss, and grass with hair and feather lining.

Eggs: Four, off-white with red-brown marks, 0.6 inch.

In summer, the black-throated green warbler often shares its coniferous woods with other insect-eating warblers. Each has adapted to permit a fair division: The warblers hunt at different tree levels to catch particular insects. This way, there are plenty of non-hairy caterpillars at the outer middle tree level for the black-throated green warbler to eat.

CHESTNUT-SIDED WARBLER | *Dendroica pensylvanica*

Size: 5 inches.

Characteristics: Chestnut flanks on pale underside. Breeding adult, dark-streaked back, yellow cap, and white face with black eyeline and moustache.

Voice: Accented (last two syllables) and unaccented "pleased-pleased-pleased-to-meet-cha."

Nest: Loose cup of bark and plant down in tree or shrub.

Eggs: Four, whitish with brown blotches, 0.7 inch.

The male chestnut-sided warbler has two versions to its song—one accented, one unaccented. By varying its intonation on this one song, it effectively increases its vocabulary to convey two messages. One version generally warns rival males against entering his territory. With a change in intonation, this aggressive song becomes an invitation to females to mate. The technique is not uncommon; other warblers also use it.

MAGNOLIA WARBLER | *Dendroica magnolia*

Size: 5 inches.

Characteristics: Breeding adult, dark with yellow underside, heavily streaked on male. Black face with white eyebrow; white wing patch and tail patch.

Voice: Musical "weety-weety-weety-wee" song.

Nest: Loose cup of fine twigs and grasses lined with black rootlets.

Eggs: Four, white with brown and olive markings, 0.7 inch.

The name is a bit of a misnomer. First of all, like most other warblers, the magnolia doesn't warble. Second, the bird breeds in the northern coniferous forests, where it is one of the most visible warblers, foraging low in the trees, its white tail patch on display. But once, while on migration, the bird happened to be spotted by the pioneering ornithologist Alexander Wilson, who observed the bird perched on a magnolia tree. Thus, its name.

YELLOW WARBLER | *Dendroica petechia*

Size: 5 inches.

Characteristics: Yellow with olive back, wings and tail, and bold, dark eyes. Yellow wing bars and tail spots. Reddish breast streaks prominent on male.

Voice: Accented (last note) and unaccented "sweet-sweet-I-am-so-sweet" song.

Nest: Cup of grasses, milkweed stems, and cobwebs with finer lining.

Eggs: Four or five, white or pale green with speckled ends, 0.7 inch.

Each summer in the willows and alders across North America, the female yellow warbler builds her nest and lays her eggs. The nest is occasionally visited by the female cowbird who adds her own egg. The yellow warbler may respond by defiantly building a new nest floor over the eggs and laying new ones. The cowbird, undeterred, may revisit and add another egg. This can go on, with neither bird relenting. On one ducumented occasion, a yellow warbler was finally left in peace with a six-layer nest.

 YELLOW-RUMPED WARBLER | *Dendroica coronata*

Size: 5.5 inches.

Characteristics: Yellow rump and "armpits;" white tail patch. Breeding adult, black with streaked white underside, yellow crown, white (myrtle) or yellow (Audubon) throat.

Voice: Myrtle, trilled two-note song; "check" call. Audubon, warbled two-note song; "whip" call.

Nest: Cup of plant material, hair and feather lining partially covering eggs, in conifer

Eggs: Four or five, cream blotched with brown and gray, 0.7 inch.

The western and eastern populations of this warbler were once considered distinct species—the Audubon and myrtle warblers—but extensive interbreeding between the two disproved this classification. The yellow-rumped warbler is among the few birds capable of digesting wax. This rare ability allows it to winter much north of its tropical relatives, feasting through the cold months on bayberry and other fruits coated with natural waxes.

 CEDAR WAXWING | *Bombycilla cedrorum*

Size: 6.5 inches.

Characteristics: Gray-brown smooth plumage with tufted crest and black mask. Yellow-tipped tail and red waxlike wingtips.

Voice: High-pitched, thin "zeee-zeee."

Nest: Bulky cup of twigs, grasses, lichens, mosses, pine needles, and wool.

Eggs: Four or five, blue-gray, 1.3 inches.

Among the most voracious of birds, cedar waxwings feast on a diet of small, sugary fruits, supplemented only in summer with insects. The name "waxwing" comes from the bright red tips on the wing feathers, which look like blobs of sealing wax. Waxwings are gregarious birds. They typically fly in flocks of thirty to a hundred. Perched together in cedar trees or on overhead wires, they will pass berries from beak to beak. Some birds have been known to become intoxicated from over-ripe berries and actually fall from their perches.

HOUSE WREN | *Troglodytes aedon*

Size: 5 inches.

Characteristics: Gray-brown with paler underside; fine, dark barring on wings and tail; brown barring on flank.

Voice: Bubbling warble, two or three seconds in length. Sequence of brief buzzes and "churrr" calls.

Nest: Twig-based cup of soft material.

Eggs: Six or seven, white, speckled red-brown, 0.6 inch.

Ironically, this little wren is recognized in the field by its lack of fieldmarks: It is the plainest of the North American wrens, but makes up for this in personality and song. As its name implies, the house wren has often lived near human habitation, setting up house in an empty flower pot or unused shoe. The male claims this breeding ground, bouncing around it, tail erect, pausing at exposed perches to release his cascade of whistles.

MARSH WREN | *Cistothorus palustris*

Size: 5 inches.

Characteristics: Brown with darker crown, white eyebrow, and black upper back streaked with white.

Voice: Song, warble of rattles. "Chek" call often repeated in fast chatter.

Nest: Football-shaped mass of woven cattails, lined with softer material, lashed to marsh stands.

Eggs: Four or five, light brown with dark brown marks, 0.7 inch.

When it comes to protecting nests from predators, the marsh wren has an original approach. The male builds up to two dozen nests on his marshy territory. His two or three mates may each nest in one of these or build its own, leaving many nests unoccupied. The marsh wren also punctures the eggs in nearby birds' nests, creating further unoccupied nests. It has been suggested that a predator, faced with all these empty nests, finds it easier to pursue its prey elsewhere.

WINTER WREN | *Troglodytes troglodytes*

Size: 4 inches.

Characteristics: Small and plump with stubby tail. Brown with barring on paler belly and undertail.

Voice: Lengthy series of musical trills. Explosive "kimp-kimp" call.

Nest: Cavity padded with plant material, lined with hair and feathers, close to ground and near water.

Eggs: Five or six, white with red-brown flecks concentrated at large end, 0.6 inch.

Though the name "winter wren" may evoke images of this little bird shivering in the snow, the winter wren usually leaves its northern breeding grounds to winter south. Only along the Pacific coast is it a permanent resident, wintering as far north as Alaska. The winter wren is a secretive bird, scampering about, mouselike, in the understory of dense woods, foraging for insects. Occasionally, it may submerge its head in a local stream to pull out a tiny fish.

BIRDER'S RESOURCE GUIDE

This handy reference guide is filled with useful facts, lists, and information, beginning with a code of birding ethics from the American Birding Association and extending to instructions for building a feeder and a birdhouse.

AMERICAN BIRDING ASSOCIATION'S CODE OF BIRDING ETHICS

1 Promote the welfare of birds and their environment.

• Support the protection of important bird habitats.

• Avoid stressing birds or exposing them to danger; exercise restraint and caution during observation, photography, sound recording, or filming:

Limit the use of recordings and other methods of attracting birds, and never use such methods in heavily birded areas or to attract any species that is threatened, endangered, or of special concern or is rare in the area.

Keep well back from nests and nesting colonies, roosts, display areas, and important feeding sites. In such sensitive areas, if extended observation, photography, filming, or recording is needed, try to use a blind or hide, taking advantage of natural cover. Use artificial light sparingly for filming or photography, especially for close-ups.

Before advertising the presence of a rare bird, evaluate the potential for disturbance to the bird, its surroundings, and other people in the vicinity; proceed only when access can be controlled, disturbance minimized, and permission has been obtained from private landowners. Only divulge the sites of rare nesting birds to the proper conservation authorities.

Stay on roads, trails, and paths where they exist; keep habitat disturbances to a minimum.

2 Respect the law, and the rights of others.

• Do not enter private property without the owner's explicit permission.

• Follow all laws, rules, and regulations governing the use of roads and public areas, both at home and when abroad.

• Practice common courtesy in all of your contacts with other people. Your exemplary behavior will generate goodwill with birding enthusiasts and non-birders alike.

3 Ensure that any feeders, nest structures, and other artificial bird environments are safe.

• Keep dispensers, water, and food clean and free of decay or disease. Be sure to feed birds continually during periods of harsh weather.

• Maintain and routinely clean your bird nest structures.

• If you are attracting birds to an area, ensure the birds are not exposed to danger from cats and other domestic animals, or posed by artificial hazards.

4 Group birding requires special care. Each individual in the group, in addition to the obligations spelled above, has responsibilities as a group member.

• Respect the interests, rights, and skills of fellow birders, as well as people participating in other legitimate outdoor activities. Freely share your knowledge and experience, being especially helpful to novice birders.

• If you witness unethical birding conduct, assess the situation, then intervene if it seems prudent. When interceding, inform the person(s) of the inappropriate action and attempt, within reason, to have it stopped. If the behavior continues, document it and notify appropriate individuals or organizations.

• Group leader responsibilities include: serving as an ethical role model; teaching through word and example; keeping groups to a size that limits environmental effects and interference with others in the area; ensuring that group members know of and practice this code; learning and informing the group of special conditions applicable to an area being visited (such as no tape recorders allowed); and acknowledging that professional tour companies bear a special responsibility to place bird welfare and the benefits of public knowledge ahead of commercial interests. Ideally leaders should keep track of tour sightings, document unusual occurrences, and submit records to appropriate organizations.

Top Twenty Hot Spots

You can, of course, start looking for birds as soon as you step outside your own door. But there are places in North America where you will greatly increase your chances of seeing not only a great number of birds, but also rare ones to add to your life list. The hot spots shown here have been chosen both for their geographical diversity—they range all the way from the rolling plains of Kanuti, Alaska to the Florida Everglades—and for the variety of birds they offer. Some places are known for certain species; Hawk Mountain in Pennsylvania, for example, is a mecca for raptor watchers. Other spots, such as Texas' Big Bend, are home to a phenomenal array of avian life.

1 Kanuti, Alaska
Close to one and one-half million acres of rolling plains between the Kanuti and Koyukuk rivers; home to hundreds of thousands of nesting waterfowl—including greater white-fronted geese, common and hoary redpolls, golden and bald eagles, and many shorebirds.

2 Beaverhill, Alberta
Large, shallow body of water hosts 253 species, including huge flocks of waterfowl and shorebirds (40 species).

3 Pacific Rim National Park, British Columbia
Located on the west coast of Vancouver Island, the park's habitats range from seacoast to bog and muskeg. More than 250 bird species have been recorded—including harlequin ducks, northern fulmars, and black-footed albatrosses.

4 Snake River, Idaho
Home of the Snake River Birds of Prey Natural Area, the world's first sanctuary for breeding raptors—including Swainson's hawks, ferruginous hawks and golden eagles.

5 Grand Teton National Park, Wyoming
Close to three hundred species have been recorded, including whooping cranes, trumpeter swans, and sixty nesting pairs of bald eagles.

6 Point Reyes National Seashore, California
Several hundred thousand shorebirds gather at this point during fall and spring migrations; birders can spot more than two hundred species in a single day.

7 Ramsey Canyon, Arizona
Bounded on three sides by the Coronado Forest; noted for fourteen hummingbird species and rare birds such as the painted redstart and the red-faced warbler.

8 Churchill, Manitoba
Millions of shorebirds in breeding plumage mixed with sightings of polar bears. Great gray owls, three-toed woodpeckers, Smith's longspurs, tundra swans, and Ross gulls are among the most highly prized species seen.

9 Gaspé Peninsula, Quebec
Famous seabird colony on Bonaventure Island is home to thousands of nesting northern gannets, black-legged kittiwakes, and razorbills. Woods on the mainland attract boreal chickadees, Swainson's thrushes, and gray jays.

10 Grand Manaan Island, New Brunswick

Audubon came here to paint. This is one of the best spots to see jaegers, guillemots, petrels, terns, gulls, shearwaters, and Atlantic puffins.

11 Plum Island, Massachusetts
Good diversity of habitat, including extensive salt marshes that attract a variety of coastal, marsh, and land birds as well as northern species such as snow buntings and snowy owls.

12 Point Pelee, Ontario
Canada's premier birding spot attracts watchers from all over the world. Especially good in May when migrating songbirds throng here—including eastern warblers, tanagers, vireos, grosbeaks and buntings.

13 Hawk Mountain, Pennsylvania
From late August to mid-November perhaps the best place in the country to see birds of prey comprising a dozen species; impressive interpretation center.

14 Cape May, New Jersey
Best known for its shorebirds, rare migrants, and annual hawk flights. Peak time for fall migrants is late September to early October. Home of the World Series of Birding each May.

15 Okefenokee National Wildlife Refuge, Georgia
Close to 400,000 acres, including extensive flooded cypress forest. Good spot to see sandhill cranes in January, prothonotary warblers in April, and red-cockaded woodpeckers in May, as well as waterfowl and large wading birds.

16 Everglades
One of many fine spots in Florida for observing birds. (Others include Ding Darling National Wildlife Refuge on Sanibel Island, the Tamiami Trail, and Corkscrew Swamp Sanctuary.) Birders come to the Everglades to see large waterbirds such as herons, egret, ibises, and pelicans; especially sought-after birds include snail kites, white-crowned pigeons, and mangrove cuckoos.

17 Aransas Refuge, Texas
More than fifty thousand acres of mixed habitats; home to painted buntings as well as various warblers and tanagers; whooping cranes winter here. Birders can also spot roseate spoonbills along with brown and white pelicans.

18 Santa Ana Wildlife Refuge, Texas
More than 330 species recorded here, including many rare and endangered birds; good spot to see hook-billed kites, olivaceous cormorants, northern bearded tyrannulets, and white-collared seedeaters.

19 Big Bend, Texas
Home to 425 bird species—more than any other park in the United States; good variety of western species, including uncommon birds such as elf owls, Colima warblers, and Lucifer hummingbirds.

20 Hawaii
The unusual habitats of the seven Hawaiian islands are home to interesting birds—including at least thirty-six species classified as endangered, such as the Hawaiian hawk and the Molokai creeper.

Extreme Birds

Tall Customers
Cranes are the tallest flying birds. Some birds, such as this crowned crane of Tanzania, can reach a height of more than six feet.

Tiny hummingbirds that build nests the size of a thimble, 345-pound ostriches, birds that fly as high as transatlantic jetliners, falcons that divebomb after prey at more than 150 miles per hour—birds are a living testament to the design ingenuity of nature.

MOST COMMON NORTH AMERICAN BREEDING BIRD
Red-winged blackbird.

SMALLEST BIRD
Bee hummingbird: 2.25 inches long.

HEAVIEST BIRDS

• Ostrich	345 lbs
• Emu	88 lbs
• Cassowary	73 lbs
• Emperor penguin	64 lbs
• Rhea	55 lbs
• Great bustard	46 lbs
• Trumpeter swan	37 lbs
• Mute swan	35 lbs

LONGEST WINGSPAN
Wandering albatross: 132 inches.

HIGHEST FLYER
Ruppell's vulture: up to 37,000 feet.

FASTEST BIRDS*

• Racing pigeon	110 mph
• Spine-tailed swift	106 mph
• Red-breasted merganser	100 mph
• Frigatebird	95 mph
• Spur-winged goose	88 mph

The peregrine falcon has been clocked at speeds of more than 150 miles per hour in a dive. The figures above are for level flight.

FASTEST FLIGHTLESS BIRD
Ostrich: forty-five miles per hour.

BIGGEST NEST
Malleefowl: sixteen feet high, thirty-six feet wide; weighs three hundred tons.

SMALLEST EGG
Vervain hummingbird: 0.1 inch long; the bird's nest is smaller than a dime in diameter.

LONGEST BILL
Australian pelican:
up to 18.5 inches long.

LONGEST ONE-WAY MIGRATIONS
* Common tern   16, 200 mi
* Arctic tern   12, 500 mi
* Short-tailed shearwater 10, 500 mi
* Parasitic jaeger   10, 000 mi
* Baird's sandpiper   9, 600 mi
* Pectoral sandpiper   9, 600 mi
* Light-mantled sooty   9, 500 mi
* Hudsonian godwit   9, 300 mi
* Lesser yellowlegs   9, 300 mi

BIGGEST FLOCKS
Flamingoes and budgerigars:
more than one million birds at a time.

Slow Flyer
The American woodcock can fly as slowly as five miles per hour without stalling.

Food and Feeding

By selecting different seeds, these simple recipes can be changed to attract your local birds. Experiment with different seed types or mixes to see what your avian visitors prefer.

POPULAR SEED MIXTURE

Here's one tried-and-true mix for seed eaters in your backyard:
50 percent sunflower seeds
35 percent white proso millet
15 percent finely cracked corn

You can vary the combinations to find one that appeals to the birds in your yard. Some birders recommend that at least 75 percent of the seed should be black-oil sunflower type.

SUET / PEANUT BUTTER BLEND

Birds such as chickadees and nuthatches love this blend:
1 cup suet
1 cup peanut butter
3 cups cornmeal
1/2 cup flour

1. Melt suet in a saucepan over low heat.
2. Add peanut butter, stirring until melted and blended. Cool until slightly thickened.
3. In a large bowl, combine cornmeal and flour.
4. Add suet mixture and mix thoroughly. You may add items at hand, such as currants, sesame seeds, grains, or bits of rendered fat. Or, select seeds from the chart at right.

To shape, line small loaf pans with plastic wrap to make it easier to remove the blend. Pack the blend in the pans and freeze it until needed. Or, pour the blend into muffin tins until half full and freeze. Place these small cakes in suet holders. Another option is to spread the unfrozen blend on a tree trunk or onto wire mesh attached to a board.

SEED CORN BREAD

Try adding a cup of birdseed to a package of commercial cornbread mix, then prepare the mix according to the instructions. Cut the bread into pieces and crumble the pieces onto a platform feeder. Freeze the remaining portions until ready for use.

FRUITS AND VEGETABLES

Birds enjoy fruits and vegetables such as apples, grapes, raisins (soak in water overnight), oranges, nectarines, tomatoes, plums, peaches, green peppers, and broccoli. Cut items in half or into pieces. Place small fruit and vegetable pieces in wire cages, suet holders, or peanut hoppers. Or mix them with larger fruits and vegetables on platform feeders. Another option: Thread chunks of fruits and vegetables onto commercially available skewers. The blunt metal rods are safe for birds and fit into holders for "serving." Also try husking a fresh ear of corn, then hanging it up with twine.

BIRDSEED SPECIAL

2 cups bread crumbs	4-5 chopped apples
1/4 cup cornmeal	1 cup raisins
1/2 cup flour (whole wheat is best)	1 cup chunky peanut butter
1/2 cup sugar	1 cup birdseed
1/2 cup shredded cheese	1 cup suet
1 cup unsalted nuts	

Mix ingredients well. If necessary, you can add extra suet or even bacon drippings if the mixture seems too crumbly. Shape into balls and freeze, then place in a mesh bag.

SPECIES PREFERENCES

NAME	FAVORITE FOODS
BLUEBIRDS	suet, mealworms, berries
BUNTINGS	sunflower seeds, safflower, millet, cracked corn, fruit
CARDINALS	sunflower seeds, safflower
CHICKADEES	peanut kernels, sunflower seeds
CREEPERS	suet, suet mix, sunflower seeds, nuts, cracked corn, bread
DOVES	millet, sunflower seeds, milo, bread, nuts, cracked corn, niger
FINCHES	niger, sunflower seeds, millet, canary seed
GOLDFINCHES	niger, black-oil sunflower seeds
GRACKLES	sunflower seeds, safflower, millet, cracked corn, fruit
GROSBEAKS	sunflower seeds, safflower
HOUSE SPARROWS	millet, peanut kernels, suet, bread crumbs, canary seed, cracked corn
HUMMINGBIRDS	sugar water (page 95)
JAYS	unshelled peanuts, sunflower seeds, suet, cracked corn, meat scraps
JUNCOS	millet, sunflower seeds, cracked corn
KINGLETS	suet, bread products
MOCKINGBIRDS	suet, sunflower seeds, peanut butter
NUTHATCHES	suet, suet mix, sunflower seeds, nuts, cracked corn, bread
ORIOLES	sugar water (page 95), fruit pieces such as orange halves
PINE SISKINS	millet, sunflower seeds, niger
QUAILS	millet, berries, cracked corn
REDPOLLS	millet, sunflower seeds, niger
RING-NECKED PHEASANTS	cracked corn, milo, wheat
ROAD RUNNERS	meat scraps, hamburger
STARLINGS	suet, fruit, milo, wheat
TANAGERS	suet, fruit, sugar water (page 95), mealworms, bread products
THRASHERS	fruit (halved apples), mealworms
THRUSHES	suet, mealworms, berries
TITMICE	peanut kernels, sunflower seeds, suet
TOWHEES	berries, chopped fruit, canned peas, millet, sunflower seeds, cracked corn
WAXWINGS	berries, raisins, sliced apples, canned peas, currants
WHITE-CROWNED SPARROWS	millet, sunflower seeds, cracked corn
WOODPECKERS	suet, meat scraps, fruit, nuts, sunflower seeds
WRENS	suet, suet mix, millet

Classic Feeder

This hopper-style bird feeder is a classic design that works well for attracting a wide variety of birds—from jays and juncoes to grackles and grosbeaks. The hinged flat on one side makes it easy to refill. Make the feeder out of a rot-resistant wood such as cedar, or paint the wood to preserve it. The windows can be made from 1/4-inch plexiglass. Cut the grooves for the windows using a router or a table saw. The windows should rest about 5/8 inch above the feeder tray—a gap that will provide a good, even flow of feed.

Join the sides to the feeder tray by screwing from underneath. Screw Top A and Top B to the sides. Attach Top C with two hinges. Cut 45-degree bevels in the tray lips and screw them to the tray. Attach the 2x4 support to the tray from above, countersinking the screws. Use stainless-steel screws throughout to prevent rusting.

Drill a hole for the one-inch pipe in the 2x4 support. Sink the post in a one-foot hole in the ground. Add ready-mix concrete and water. Use a baffle (page 92) to keep squirrels at bay.

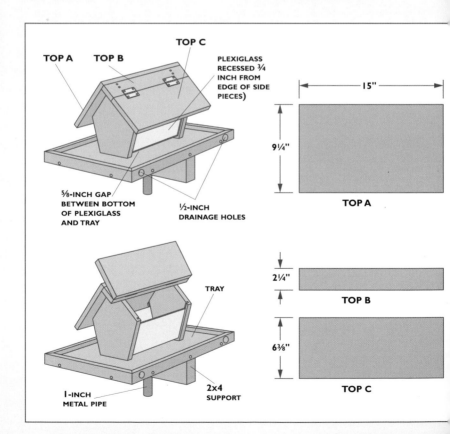

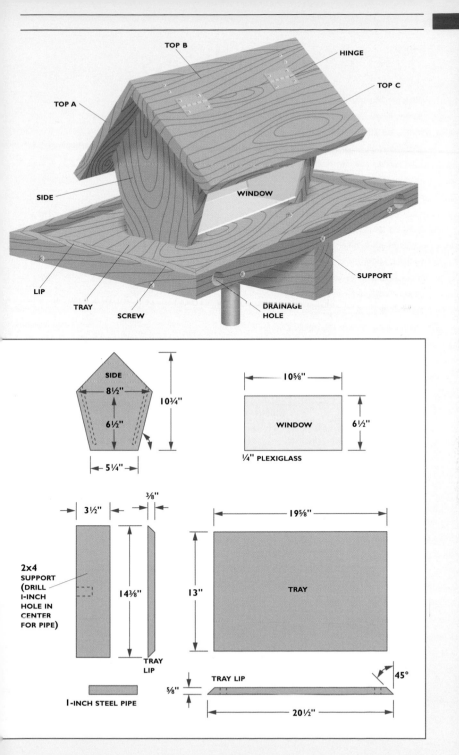

TOP B

HINGE

TOP C

TOP A

SIDE

WINDOW

SUPPORT

LIP

TRAY

SCREW

DRAINAGE HOLE

SIDE

8½"

10¾"

6½"

5¼"

10⅝"

WINDOW

6½"

¼" PLEXIGLASS

3½"

⅜"

2x4 SUPPORT (DRILL 1-INCH HOLE IN CENTER FOR PIPE)

14⅜"

TRAY LIP

19⅝"

13"

TRAY

1-INCH STEEL PIPE

TRAY LIP

⅝"

45°

20½"

The Basic Birdhouse

The birdhouse shown on these pages is designed for bluebirds, but it can be adapted to suit many birds simply by adjusting the pieces of the box to the dimensions shown in the chart below. The size of the entrance hole is critical; making it too large will allow larger unwanted species to use the birdhouse. Ledge nesters, such as robins and swallows, prefer houses with an open front. The dimensions for a purple martin house are for a single compartment of a multi-unit "apartment." For more information on birdhouse construction, see page 98.

BIRDHOUSE DIMENSIONS

SPECIES	INTERIOR FLOOR SIZE (INCHES)	DIAMETER OF ENTRANCE HOLE (INCHES)	INTERIOR HEIGHT OF BOX (INCHES)	HEIGHT ABOVE GROUND (FEET)
CHICKADEE	4x4	$1\frac{1}{8}$	10	6-15
WOOD DUCK	12x12	3x4	24	5-20
NORTHERN FLICKER	7x7	$2\frac{1}{2}$	16-24	10-20
GREAT-CRESTED FLYCATCHER	6x6	2	18	8-20
PURPLE MARTIN	6x6	$2\frac{1}{4}$	6	15-20
NUTHATCH	4x4	$1\frac{3}{8}$	12	6-12
SCREECH OWL	8x8	3	18	10-30
PHOEBE	6x6	open front	6	8-12
ROBIN	6x8	open front	8	6-15
BARN SWALLOW	6x6	open front	6	6-12
TITMOUSE	4x4	$1\frac{1}{2}$	12	6-15
DOWNY WOODPECKER	4x4	$1\frac{3}{8}$	12	6-20
HAIRY WOODPECKER	6x6	$1\frac{1}{2}$-2	14	10-20
BEWICK'S WREN	4x4	$1\frac{1}{4}$	11	6-10
CAROLINA WREN	4x4	$1\frac{1}{2}$	12	6-10
HOUSE WREN	4x4	1	11	6-10

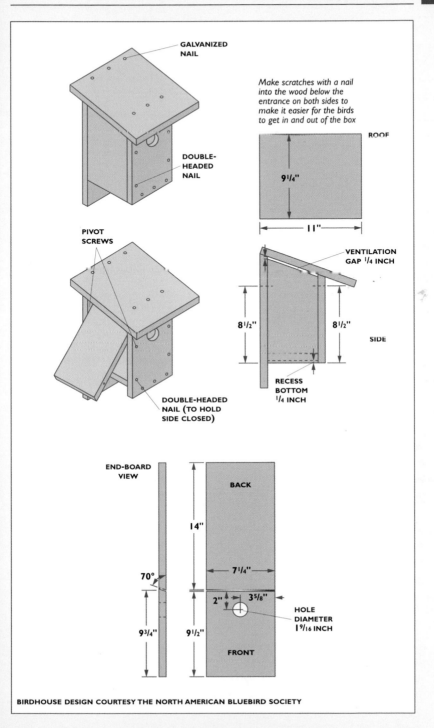

GALVANIZED NAIL

DOUBLE-HEADED NAIL

PIVOT SCREWS

DOUBLE-HEADED NAIL (TO HOLD SIDE CLOSED)

Make scratches with a nail into the wood below the entrance on both sides to make it easier for the birds to get in and out of the box

ROOF

9¼"

11"

VENTILATION GAP ¼ INCH

8½"

8½"

SIDE

RECESS BOTTOM ¼ INCH

END-BOARD VIEW

BACK

14"

7¼"

70°

2" 3⅝"

HOLE DIAMETER 1⁹⁄₁₆ INCH

9¾"

9½"

FRONT

BIRDHOUSE DESIGN COURTESY THE NORTH AMERICAN BLUEBIRD SOCIETY

Important Addresses

LUBS AND ASSOCIATIONS

American Birding Association
Box 6599
Colorado Springs, CO 80934
719-578-9703

Association of Field Ornithologists
c/o Allen Press
P.O. Box 1897
Lawrence, KS 66044-1897

The Colonial Waterbird Society
Savannah River Ecology Lab
Drawer E
Aiken, SC 29802
803-952-7451
E-mail: bryan@srel.edu

The Cornell Laboratory of Ornithology
159 Sapsucker Woods Rd.
Ithaca, NY 14850
607-254-2425

Georgia Ornithological Society
P.O. Box 1684
Cartersville, GA 30120

Great Basin Bird Observatory (GBBO)
440 Hill Street, Suite D
Reno, Nevada 89501
702-348-2644
Fax: 702-329-6825
E-mail: GChisholm@aol.com

Hawk Migration Association of North America
4304 Santa Anna Dr.
Columbia, MO 65201

Inland Bird Banding Association
R.D. 2, Box 26
Wisner, NE 68791

International Crane Foundation (ICF)
E-11376, Shady Lane Rd.
Baraboo, WI 53913

Kirkland Bird Club
Box 14
Yorkville, NY 13495

Louisiana Ornithological Society
504 Whitebark Dr.
Lafayette, LA 70508
318-988-4898

Maryland Ornithological Society, Inc.
Cylburn Mansion
4915 Greenspring Ave.
Baltimore, MD 21209
800-823-0050

National Audubon Society
700 Broadway
New York, NY 10003
212-979-3117

North American Bluebird Society
P.O. Box 74
Darlington, WI 53530-0074
608-329-6403

Purple Martin Conservation Association
Edinboro University of Pennsylvania
Edinboro, PA 16444
814-734-4420
E-mail: pmca@edinboro.edu

Roger Tory Peterson Institute of Natural History
311 Curtis St.
Jamestown, NY 14701
716-665-2473

The International Osprey Foundation
P.O. Box 250
Sanibel Island, FL 33957-0250

The Nature Conservancy
4245 N. Fairfax Dr.
Arlington, VA 22203
703-841-5300

The Peregrine Fund
566 W. Flying Hawk Lane
Boise, ID 83709
208-362-3716
E-mail: tpf@peregrinefund.org

The Ruffed Grouse Society
451 McCormick Rd.
Coraopolis, PA 15108

The Trumpeter Swan Society
3800 County Rd. 24
Maple Plain, MN 55359

Virginia Society of Ornithology
520 Rainbow Forest Dr.
Lynchburg, VA 24502

Washington Ornitholgical Society
P.O. Box 31783
Seattle, WA 98103-1783

World Owl Trust
The Owl Centre
Muncaster Castle
Ravenglass
Cumbria, CA18 1RQ
England
E-mail: admin@owls.org

BIRDING HOTLINES

Hotlines are often staffed by volunteers, so they may change frequently. To find active hotlines, contact your local chapter of the National Audubon Society.

North American Rare Bird Alert (NARBA) 800-458-BIRD provides information on rare sightings across North America.

Alabama: 205-987-2730

Alaska: 907-338-2473

Arizona
Phoenix: 602-832-8745
Tucson: 520-798-1005

Arkansas: 501-753-5853

California
North: 415-681-7422
Santa Barbara: 805-964-8240
Los Angeles: 213-874-1318

Colorado: 303-424-2144

Connecticut: 203-254-3665

Delaware: 302-658-2747

District of Columbia: 301-652-1088

Florida: 561-340-0079

Georgia: 770-493-8862

Idaho
North: 208-882-6195
Southeast: 208-236-3337
Southwest: 208-368-6096

Illinois
Central: 217-785-1083
Chicago: 847-265-2118

Indiana: 317-259-0911

Iowa: 319-338-9881

Kansas: 316-229-2777

Kentucky: 502-894-9538

Louisiana
Baton Rouge: 504-768-9874
Southeast: 504-834-2473
Southwest: 318-988-9898

Maine: 207-781-2332

Maryland: 301-652-1088

Massachusetts
East: 781-259-8805
Cape Cod: 508-349-9464
West: 413-253-2218

Michigan: 616-471-4919

Minnesota: 612-780-8890

Missouri: 573-445-9115

Montana: 406-721-9799

Nebraska: 402-292-5325

Nevada
Northwest: 702-324-2473
South: 702-390-8463

New Hampshire: 603-224-9900

New Jersey: 908-766-2661

New Mexico: 505-323-9323

New York
Albany: 518-439-8080
New York City: 212-979-3070

North Carolina: 704-332-2473

North Dakota: 701-250-4481

Ohio
Cincinnati: 513-521-2847
Columbus: 614-221-9736

Oklahoma: 918-669-6646

Oregon: 503-292-0661

Pennsylvania
East: 610-252-3455
Central: 717-255-1212 ext. 5761
Philadelphia: 215-567-2473

Rhode Island: 401-949-3870

South Carolina: 704-332-2473

South Dakota: 605-773-6460

Tennessee: 615-356-7636

Texas: 713-964-5867

Utah: 801-538-4730

Vermont: 802-457-2779

Virginia: 757-238-2713

Washington: 425-454-2662

West Virginia: 304-736-3086

Wisconsin: 414-352-3857

Wyoming: 307-265-2473

REHABILITATION CENTERS

To find the name of a bird rehabilitation center near you, contact your local Fish and Game Department, veterinarian, or Humane Society.

Bibliography

As the second most popular hobby in America (after gardening), bird-watching is a subject that attracts considerable attention from various media. Here is a brief sampling of what's available in the way of general books, field guides, online, and multimedia.

GENERAL BOOKS

Bird Photography Pure and Simple
by Arthur Morris

Equipment, film choice, composition, and techniques on getting close to the subject, along with thirty color photographs.

Bird Watching for Dummies,
by Bill Thompson (Editor of *Bird Watcher's Digest*)

An excellent wide-ranging guide for the person who knows little about birds except what he sees out his windows. The book is basic enough that the neophyte can start from zero and work his way up, but organized in a way that a more experienced birder can find worthwhile information and advice, too.

Bird Song: Identification Made Easy
by Ernie Jardine

A field guide to the songs of 125 of the more common birds of eastern North America. Helps the birder identify a song in the field without the immediate aid of audio tapes or CDs.

Bald Eagle
by Gordon Morrison

Amply illustrated by the author, who has provided drawings for several Peterson's guides. Focuses on younger readers, but discusses birds with relative depth.

Down and Dirty Birding
by Joey Slinger

Subtitled *From the Sublime to the Ridiculous— Here's All the Outrageous but True Stuff You've Ever Wanted to Know About North American Birds*, this irreverent book is a guide to looking, acting, and talking like a knowledgeable expert on avian life.

The Birder's Sourcebook
by Sheila Buff

A compilation of hundreds of addresses and telephone numbers of interest to birders in the U.S. and Canada, with information ranging from workshops and courses to museums and libraries.

The Bird Almanac
by David M. Bird

A collection of essential facts and figures from the world of birds; includes a checklist of all known birds worldwide, tabulated facts on physiology, reproduction, and mortality, plus a who's who in the fields of bird biology and conservation.

The Bird Garden
(National Audubon Society); by Stephen W. Kress

Provides a wealth of advice on choosing and maintaining plants that attract birds. Includes information on nesting and year-round feeding. Offers a guide to common birds and recommended plants.

The Bird Feeder Book
by Donald and Lillian Stokes

This guide helps readers not only learn how to attract more birds, but also become more proficient at identifying birds and understanding their behaviors. The authors write a regular column that appears in *Bird Watcher's Digest*.

The Birder's Handbook: A Field Guide to the Natural History of North American Birds
by Paul Ehrlich, Darryl Wheye, and David S. Dobkin

A wealth of interesting, up-to-date information on everything from why birds fly in V-formation to camouflage techniques. Profiles of more than six hundred birds that breed in North America.

Lives of North American Birds
by Kenn Kaufman

Provides detailed information about how birds live, how long eggs take to hatch, what birds eat, where birds go in the winter, and more.

FIELD GUIDES

Field Guide to the Birds of Eastern and Central North America
by Roger Tory Peterson
Written by the man who pioneered field guides. Includes birds found east of the hundredth meridian.

A Field Guide to Western Birds
by Roger Tory Peterson
Covers all the birds in western North America.

Stokes Field Guide to Birds
(Stokes Field Guides) by Donald and Lillian Stokes
Good for beginners; easy-to-use identification guide. The book is available in two editions: one covering the birds in Eastern North America; the other covers birds found in the West.

National Geographic Society Field Guide to the Birds of North America
Comprehensive guide. A good choice for experienced birders.

The Audubon Society Field Guide to North American Birds
An all-photographic field guide. The photos are organized according to silhouette and color, while the text is arranged by habitat. The book is available in an Eastern- and Western-region version. A good beginners' guide, with enough information to satisfy the more experienced birder.

ONLINE

The plethora of information on the World Wide Web offers a treasure trove of information for birders. However, web addresses often change, so we have listed only bird related domain names in this guide. To find new web sites, use terms such as birding, bird feeder, and the like in web search engines.

www.birders.com
A useful site with international links and a focus on Hawaiian and Pacific birding.

www.americanbirding.org
The web site of the American Birding Association. Provides much useful information for birders, as well as links to other sites on the web.

http://birding.mining-co.com/
A comprehensive commercial site, featuring a weekly newsletter and links to national and international birding organizations.

MULTIMEDIA

Birds of North America 2.0 CD-ROM
(Thayer Software)
Multimedia field guide containing more than 2,800 photos and almost seven hundred songs. Includes *The Birder's Handbook*. Also includes side-by-side comparisons, 121 videos, sonograms, a bird finder, and links to hot birding websites.

Eyewitness Virtual Reality Bird CD-ROM
(Dorling Kindersley Books)
Covers the scientific and historical aspects of birds. Learn how birds sing. Compare songs. Birds-Eye View lets you see what things look like through the eyes of different birds.

National Audubon Society CD-ROM
(Random House)
Pictures, sounds, games, etc. Use your computer and this CD-ROM to learn bird songs, practice your identification skills, and learn about habitats and bird behavior.

How to Start Watching Birds: Your Lifetime Ticket to the Theater of Nature
(Video, ninety minutes)
Covers the basics of bird identification. Provides tips and techniques useful for the beginner.

A Celebration of Birds with Roger Tory Peterson (Video, fifty-four minutes)
by Judy Fieth and Michael Male
This multiple award-winning film takes the viewer on several birding trips with Roger Tory Peterson. While watching birds in Florida, Maine, and Connecticut, Roger talks about his early birding career (with interesting black-and-white footage of Roger as a teen birder) and the conservation issues facing North American birders today.

Index

Text references are in plain type;
illustrations in italic;
*photographs in **boldface**;*
bird biographies in italic
with asterisk (*).

tanagers, 90-91
tarsus, *109*
taste, 26-27
taxonomy, 104-105
   See also classification
teal, green-winged, *133**
teeth
   egg tooth, 57
   elimination of, 16
telephone hotlines, 183
temperature
   body, 11
   of eggs, 51, 57
   regulation, warm-blooded
      adults and cold-blooded
      young, 58
temporal resolution, 24
tern, Arctic, *135**
   migration, 65, 67, 67, 175
tern, common, *135**, 175
tern, least, 50
tern, white, 50
terns
   identifying, 106, *135**
   wings, 40, *41*
territories, *60*, 60-61
thermal soaring, 34, *34*, 41
thrasher, brown, *165**
   courtship, 48
   wing markings, *113*
thrashers, 88
thrush, hermit, 112, *165**
thrush, wood, 112, *165**
titmice, 18, 180
titmouse, tufted, *166**
toes, 12, *13*
tongues, 27, *27*
tool use, 18
touch, 28-29
towhee, eastern, *166**
   tail markings, *113*
toxins. *See* poisons
trachea, *10*, 11, *72*
tracking, 68, 68-69, *69*
trees, 86, 86-89, *88*
turkey, wild, 48, *142**

U-V

urine, 17
vane, *37*
vascular system, 11
vegetables, 176, 177
Velociraptor, 8
vent, *16*, 17
ventriculus, 16
videos, 185
vireo, red-eyed, *166**
   eye markings, *112*
vireos, 52

vision, 20-23
   binocular, 21, *21*
   color, 22-23
   eyes, 10, 20, 20-23, *22*
   field of vision, 20, 21, *21*
   focusing, 20, 21
   light wavelengths, 23
   monocular, 21
   nictitating membranes,
      23, *23*
   360° vision, *21*
vocal appropriation, 158
vocal system, *72*, 72-73
vocalizations
   calls, 70
   duet singing, 71
   identifying birds by,
      112-113
   mimicry, *74*, 74, 74-75, *75*
   recording, 73, *73*, *74*, 85, *85*
   song analysis, 73, *73*
   songs, 70, *70*, 71-72
   of specific birds, 120-169
   spectrograms, 73, *73*, *74*
   "talking," 19, *19*, 75
   vocal system, *72*, 72-73
   See also nonvocal
      communication
vulture, black, 111
vulture, Ruppell's, 174
vulture, turkey, 26, 111, *138**

W

waders, small, 106, *121**-*126**
wading birds, long-legged,
   106, *126**-*128**
wagtail, yellow, 61
warbler, black-and-white, 113
warbler, black-throated green,
   167*
warbler, chestnut-sided, 110,
   167*
warbler, magnolia, *167**
warbler, marsh, 74
warbler, prairie, 59
warbler, red, 52
warbler, reed, 53
warbler, wood, 112
warbler, yellow, 52, 113, *168**
warbler, yellow-rumped, 110,
   168*
warblers
   attracting, 88
   and brood parasitism, 52
   foot, *13*
waste materials, 17, *17*
   fecal sacs, 59
waxwing, cedar, *168**
   diet, 86
   wing markings, *113*
waxwings, 87-88
weaver, village, 19
weaverbird, 51

webs, 12, *13*
weight extremes, 174
whip-poor-will, 14, 38, *140**
windows, preventing crashes
   into, 23
wings
   longest wingspan, 174
   markings, *113*
   shape, 30, 31
   size in diving waterfowl, 32
   size in flightless birds, 32-33
   types, 40-41, *41*
   wingspan, 120-169, 174
   See also feathers; flight
winter
   birdbaths, 96
   and blood flow in feet, 12
woodcock, American, *126**,
   175
woodcocks
   vision, *21*
woodpecker, downy, 180
woodpecker, hairy, 112, *144**,
   180
woodpecker, pileated, 14, *145**
woodpecker, red-bellied, 112
woodpecker, red-headed, 61,
   145*, 175
woodpecker, white-headed
   tongue, *27*
woodpeckers
   bathing, 43
   beak, *14*, 15
   feeding, 91
   foot, *13*
   tail, 41, 44
   touch receptors, 28
   wings, 40
wood-pewee, eastern, *160**
wren, Bewick's, 180
wren, Carolina, *100*, 180
wren, Central American, 71
wren, house, *169**
   birdhouse, 180
   feeding young, 59
   winter habitat, 111
wren, marsh, 70, *169**
   nest, *51*
wren, winter, *169**
wrens, 59
wrynecks
   tongue, *27*

X-Y-Z

yellowlegs, greater, *128**
yellowlegs, lesser, 175
young
   altricial, 58, 58, 59
   brooding, 58, 58-59
   defending, 59
   feeding, 16, **17**, 58, 58-59
   precocial, 58, 58

ST. REMY MULTIMEDIA

President: Pierre Léveillé
Vice-President, Finance: Natalie Watanabe
Managing Editor: Carolyn Jackson
Managing Art Director: Diane Denoncourt
Production Manager: Michelle Turbide
Director, Business Development: Christopher Jackson
Senior Editor: Pierre Home-Douglas
Art Director: Solange Laberge
Contributing Art Director: Philippe Arnoldi
Researcher/Writers: Steve Krolak, Kat Rother,
  Rebecca Smollett
Designer: Hélène Dion
Illustrators: Ronald DuRepos, François Escalmel,
  Patrick Jougla, Jacques Perrault, Maryo Proulx
Photo Researcher: Linda Castle
Researcher: Adam Van Sertima
Indexer: Linda Cardella Cournoyer
Senior Editor: Production: Brian Parsons
Systems Director: Edward Renaud
Technical Support: Jean Sirois
Scanner Operators: Martin Francoeur,
  Sara Grynspan

ACKNOWLEDGMENTS

The editors wish to thank the following:
Allan J. Baker, Centre for Biodiversity and
  Conservation Biology, Royal Ontario Museum;
George Constable, for his editorial contributions;
Joel Cracraft, Department of Ornithology,
  American Museum of Natural History;
Ari Epstein, Scientific American Explorations;
Barrie Frost, Department of Psychology, Queen's
  University, Kingston;
Mark Fuller, Raptor Research Center, Boise State
  University;
Paul Green, American Birding Association;
Prof. Robert Lemon, Department of Biology,
  McGill University;
Peter Marler, Center for Animal Behavior,
  University of California, Davis;
Lisa Marokis, Service Argos Inc.;
Douglas A. Nelson, Borror Laboratory of
  Bioacoustics, Ohio State University;
Irene Pepperberg, Department of Ecology and
  Evolutionary Biology, University of Arizona;
Carol Schwartz, Banting and Best Dept. of
  Medical Research, University of Toronto;
Richard Wagner, Biology Department, York
  University, Toronto;
Tamaki Yuri, Museum of Zoology, University of
  Michigan;
Robert M. Zink, J. F. Bell Museum of Natural
  History, University of Minnesota.

*The following persons also assisted in
the preparation of this book:*
Neale McDevitt, Laird Greenshields, Maryse
Doray, Michel Giguère, Anne-Marie Lemay,
and Robert Chartier.

PICTURE CREDITS

Robert McKemie/Daybreak Imagery-6, 7, O.
Louis Mazzatenta/National Geographic Image
Collection-8, E.R. Degginger/Photo Researchers,
Inc.-9, Tom J. Ulrich- 12, 59, 71, 94, Art Wolfe-15,
32, 114-c, 115-e, David W. Harp/Folio, Inc.-17
(upper), Breck P. Kent/Animals Animals-17
(lower), Tui De Roy/Bruce Coleman Inc.-18, 56,
William Munoz-19, Jack A. Barrie/Bruce
Coleman Inc.-20, Richard Day/Daybreak
Imagery-23, 30, 48, 58 (lower), 76, 77, 90, 98, 101
(both), 175 (upper), Juan Manuel Renjifo/Animals
Animals-24, Barrie Frost, Department of
Psychology, Queen's University, Kingston, Ont.-25,
Joe McDonald/Bruce Coleman Inc.-26, Dr. Eckart
Pott/Bruce Coleman Inc.-28, Arthur
Morris/BIRDS AS ART-29 (both), 40, 45, 49, 52
(lower), 64, 70, 82, 83, 84, 85 (upper), 110, 111,
Stephen Dalton/Photo Researchers, Inc.-31, Scott
Nielsen/Bruce Coleman Inc.-33, 42, 46, 47,
Andrew Syred/Science Photo Library/Photo
Researchers, Inc.-37 (both), R.K. Bowers/
VIREO-38 (left), P.B.Connors/VIREO-38 (right)
S. & S. Rucker/VIREO-58 (inset), Maslowski
Photo-39 (upper), 43 (lower), 58 (upper), 80, 96,
97, 100, 102, 103, Ken Graham/Bruce Coleman
Inc.-43 (upper), Laura Riley/Bruce Coleman Inc.-
44, John Markham/Bruce Coleman Inc.-52
(upper), Roger Wilmshurst/Bruce Coleman Inc.-
53, David Madison/Bruce Coleman Inc.-62, 63,
Jack Dermid/Bruce Coleman Inc.-63 (upper),
Jonathan Blair/National Geographic Image
Collection-66, Richard & Susan Day/Animals
Animals-66, 67, John Hyde/Bruce Coleman Inc.-
67, Tom Maechtle-68, Professor Robert Lemon,
McGill University-73, Ken Cole/Animals
Animals-74, Hans Reinhard/Bruce Coleman Inc.-
75, Robert Chartier-39 (lower), 78, 91 (all), 93, 95,
Henry Horenstein/Corbis -Bettmann-79, Jack
Wilburn/Animals Animals-85 (lower), Richard
Shiell/Animals Animals-86, Kit Walling/Folio,
Inc.-88, John Gerlach/Earth Scenes-114 (A), Rolf
Kopfle/KOPFL/Bruce Coleman Inc.-114 (B),
Robert Falls/Bruce Coleman Inc.-115 (A), Charles
Palek/Earth Scenes-115 (B), Wendell
Metzen/Bruce Coleman Inc.-115 (C), John
Shaw/Bruce Coleman Inc.-115 (D), Jeff
Foott/Bruce Coleman Inc.-116, Gordon & Cathy
Illg/Animals Animals-117 (upper), Lynn M.
Stone/Bruce Coleman Inc.-117 (lower), Frank
Krahmer/KRAHM/Bruce Coleman Inc.-174, Gary
Meszaros/Bruce Coleman Inc.-175 (lower).